CAMBRIDGE
UNIVERSITY PRESS

CAMBRIDGE PRIMARY
Global Perspectives

Teacher's Resource 6
Adrian Ravenscroft & Thomas Holman

CAMBRIDGE
UNIVERSITY PRESS

University Printing House, Cambridge CB2 8BS, United Kingdom

One Liberty Plaza, 20th Floor, New York, NY 10006, USA

477 Williamstown Road, Port Melbourne, VIC 3207, Australia

314–321, 3rd Floor, Plot 3, Splendor Forum, Jasola District Centre, New Delhi – 110025, India

79 Anson Road, #06–04/06, Singapore 079906

Cambridge University Press is part of the University of Cambridge.

It furthers the University's mission by disseminating knowledge in the pursuit of education, learning and research at the highest international levels of excellence.

www.cambridge.org
Information on this title: www.cambridge.org/9781108926867

First published 2021

20 19 18 17 16 15 14 13 12 11 10 9 8 7 6 5 4 3 2 1

Printed in Great Britain by Ashford Colour Press Ltd.

A catalogue record for this publication is available from the British Library

ISBN 978-1-108-92686-7 Teacher's Resource 6 Paperback with Digital Access

Additional resources for this publication at www.cambridge.org/GO

Cover illustration: Omar Aranda (Beehive Illustration). Photos in downloadable 4.4: p.1 pskeltonphoto/Getty Images; p.2 Max Labeille/Getty Images; p.3 Tolimir/Getty Images; p.4 Ivan Spasic/EyeEm/Getty Images

〉 Contents

Introduction   v

How to use this Teacher's Resource   vii

Approaches to learning and teaching   ix

Section 1 Research   1
Starting with research skills: Lesson 1   2
Starting with research skills: Lesson 2   3
Starting with research skills: Lesson 3   5
Developing research skills: Lesson 4   7
Developing research skills: Lesson 5   9
Developing research skills: Lesson 6   11
Getting better at research skills: Lesson 7   13
Getting better at research skills: Lesson 8   14
Getting better at research skills: Lesson 9   16

Section 2 Analysis   18
Starting with analysis skills: Lesson 1   19
Starting with analysis skills: Lesson 2   21
Starting with analysis skills: Lesson 3   23
Developing analysis skills: Lesson 4   25
Developing analysis skills: Lesson 5   26
Developing analysis skills: Lesson 6   28
Getting better at analysis skills: Lesson 7   31
Getting better at analysis skills: Lesson 8   33
Getting better at analysis skills: Lesson 9   34

Section 3 Evaluation   37
Starting with evaluation skills: Lesson 1   38
Starting with evaluation skills: Lesson 2   40
Developing evaluation skills: Lesson 3   42
Developing evaluation skills: Lesson 4   43
Getting better at evaluation skills: Lesson 5   45

Section 4 Reflection   47
Starting with reflection skills: Lesson 1   48
Starting with reflection skills: Lesson 2   50
Starting with reflection skills: Lesson 3   52
Developing reflection skills: Lesson 4   53
Developing reflection skills: Lesson 5   55
Developing reflection skills: Lesson 6   57
Getting better at reflection skills: Lesson 7   59

Getting better at reflection skills: Lesson 8   61
Getting better at reflection skills: Lesson 9   63

Section 5 Collaboration   65
Starting with collaboration skills: Lesson 1   66
Starting with collaboration skills: Lesson 2   67
Developing collaboration skills: Lesson 3   69
Developing collaboration skills: Lesson 4   71
Getting better at collaboration skills: Lesson 5   73

Section 6 Communication   75
Starting with communication skills: Lesson 1   76
Starting with communication skills: Lesson 2   77
Developing communication skills: Lesson 3   78
Developing communication skills: Lesson 4   80
Getting better at communication skills: Lesson 5   82

Digital resources

⤓ The following items are available on Cambridge GO. For more information on how to access and use your digital resource, please see front cover.

Active learning

Assessment for learning

Developing learners' language skills

Differentiation

Improving learning through questioning

Language awareness

Metacognition

Skills for life

Downloadable worked examples and activity templates

> Introduction

Cambridge Primary Global Perspectives is an innovative programme designed to help learners develop a range of key skills that equip them to understand the processes shaping our complex, fast-changing and inter-connected world. It's crucial learners have the opportunity to develop and apply their growing skills to real issues that they experience in their communities. At the heart of the course is a varied and active learning approach, which inspires learners to explore a wide range of issues, different points of view and how to make practical changes.

This approach underpins each learner's skills book and teacher's book and is structured around six skills: research, analysis, evaluation, reflection, collaboration and communication. Each skills section follows the same approach, with friendly characters guiding learners through a 'Starting with', 'Developing' and 'Getting better at' scaffold, building their awareness of their own progress and encouraging them as they learn to take charge of their own learning journey.

A range of activities and tasks are included, with plenty of opportunities for peer-to-peer and group work, and to encourage learners to reflect on progress, track action and achievements and record their next steps. The self-assessment activities build on each other to give learners a clear record of how they are progressing, and these will help you to support them in their learning journey whilst maintaining an overview of any gaps in knowledge and understanding. The learner's skills books are write-in resources, so each learner can create and keep a portfolio of their work and track their progression through each skill and each stage. The first part of this teacher's book includes useful guidance around teaching techniques and pedagogical approaches.

Tips on providing support and challenge for learners are provided throughout. Lesson ideas are designed to help you plan for each stage of your lesson, motivate learners and monitor their progress against learning goals. Worked examples are included for each lesson to illustrate how to build and teach a skill through a relevant Cambridge Global Perspectives issue, using sample material and exemplars. Exemplars are provided to give you an idea of 'What A Good One Looks Like.' Learners' progress should be evaluated by how they demonstrate essential concepts, knowledge, skills and principles of Cambridge Global Perspectives. This selection of real-life and fictional examples is there to help you plan, but is in no way intended to be a 'correct' way of working through the skills – the ideas are intended to be flexible, and we hope they will assist you in generating ideas to apply to the topic you are working on.

All of the skills are carefully modelled through the learner's skills book and worked examples, and you can adapt them appropriately so your learners can successfully contextualise within their own community. Rather than using the exemplar materials from the teacher's resource directly with learners, use them to develop the range of parallels, examples, expositions and demonstrations that you can use relevant to your context.

By using our scaffolded approach through each skill and each stage, we think that you will find a solid framework on which to build. The scaffolded approach will support learners with English as an Additional Language. Where learners have prior experience of the Stage 5 materials, cognitive load is further managed by learners applying similar skills to different contexts in order to consolidate them. Learners who are learning English as a second language will need additional scaffolding when using these materials and would likely benefit from opportunities to explore issues in their first language. Consult senior staff and school policies to ascertain your school's perspective on best practice.

We hope to support you as an effective facilitator of Cambridge Global Perspectives, showing your learners where to look but not what to see, and helping them to enjoy exploring ideas in the classroom and in the community. We hope you will find this process of growing empowered reflective and engaged global citizens a rewarding one.

Cambridge Global Perspectives involves learners in learning about the world around them; the impact of global issues on their local area and different perspectives on how best to resolve these issues. You may need to involve learners in communicating with people in the wider community, conducting research off-site and exchanging ideas with learners in contrasting settings. All off-site visits must be risk assessed and carried out in accordance with relevant school health and safety policies. All communication must be conducted in line with school safeguarding and e-safety policies.

> How to use this Teacher's Resource

This Teacher's Resource contains both general guidance and teaching notes that help you to deliver the content in Cambridge Primary Global Perspectives Stage 6.

There are teaching notes for each lesson of the Learner's Skills Book. Each set of teaching notes contains the following features to help you deliver the unit.

At the start of each section there is a table of **cross-curricular links** and **topics modelled**, to give a clear oversight of coverage and potential use within each skill.

SKILLS SECTION	CROSS-CURRICULAR LINKS *Learners have opportunities to apply their knowledge and understanding of, and skills in:*	TOPICS MODELLED
Starting with	Geography: human geography • Understanding human characteristics of places Language skills: speaking and listening • Listen, reflect on what is heard and give a reasoned response with reference to at least one specific point made by the speaker	Moving goods and people Reduce, re-use,

At the start of each lesson is a summary of the relevant **learning objectives** and **learning goals** for the lesson. The learning objective feature takes the objectives from the curriculum framework and the lesson learning goals feature takes the more learner friendly goals as they are set out in the Learner's Skills Book.

Reflecting the activities in the Learner's Skills Book, each lesson consists of advice on how to work through the **Prior learning** activity, **Starter activity**, **Main activity**, **Class discussion** and **Peer assessment**. To help you plan, a suggested time is given against each element of the lesson, and a list of **resources** you will need has been included with each lesson.

The **Prior learning** activities allow you to build on learners' previous knowledge ready to move forward in the skill development.

CAMBRIDGE STAGE 6 RESEARCH LEARNING OBJECTIVES

1.1 Constructing research questions: Begin to construct research questions with support

LESSON LEARNING GOALS

To start to:

• say what a global issue is

• identify different types of question

• make my own questions to help me understand global issues.

Prior learning (approx. 5–10 mins)

Good for: Building on previous knowledge.

Activity: Ask learners to discuss what 'global issues' means.

Ways of working: Give learners time to discuss global issues in pairs or small groups before staging a plenary session in which learners share and respond to each other's ideas.

The ideas for the **Starter activity** are designed to grab your learners' attention and create interest and engagement. They include advice on what to listen out for, how to diagnose issues and how to make decisions about what to do next.

Starter activity (approx. 10–15 mins)

Good for: Starting to understand the difference between local and global issues, and how they may be inter-related; identifying different types of questions that can be asked about an issue.

Activity: Read through the learning goals for this lesson with learners at the beginning of this activity. After looking at an example, ask learners to identify another local issue that has global dimensions and complete a table by listing some of the problems it causes.

The **Main activity** ideas give instructions for successful execution of the activity, with differentiation advice, suggestions for feedback and answers where relevant.

Main activity (approx. 20–25 mins)

Good for: Helping learners to start identifying different types of question that can be asked about an issue and making up their own questions to develop a deeper understanding of it.

Activity: After looking at an example of how a mind-map can be used to generate questions about an issue, ask learners to identify different types of question as local, national or global. Then ask them to choose a different topic and make up their own questions about it, following this model.

Suggested answers are given in each lesson for the each of these activities. Where appropriate, there is also a **Worked Example** for the Starter activity or Main activity, to demonstrate how the activity could work with a relevant Challenge topic. This serves as an example of what success looks like, but you do not have to use the topic given in the example. These Worked Examples are provided as downloadables.

Worked Example for the Main activity

	Local question	National question	Global question
What gets thrown away in our school?	✓		
What does the law say?		✓	
What problems does waste cause our planet?			✓
Where's the nearest recycling place?	✓		
What can be recycled in our country?		✓	
How can the government help?		✓	
What's the best way people can cut down on waste?			✓
What problems does waste cause in our area?	✓		

At the end of each sub section (Starting with, Developing, Getting better at), there is advice on **Taking it further**. This contains ideas on how to draw on, go deeper into and get creative with the ideas presented each lesson.

Taking it further: Lessons 1–3

How do your learners travel to school? Based on their work in Lesson 2, encourage learners to think of the pros and cons of each method of travel that is used by their classmates. Stage a debate, with learners arguing in favour of their preferred method of travel, pointing out its advantages and the disadvantages of other methods.

Register to access free supporting resources through Cambridge GO – the home for all of your Cambridge digital content. Visit cambridge.org/go

⟩ Approaches to learning and teaching

The following are the teaching approaches underpinning our course content and how we understand and define them.

Active Learning

Active learning is a teaching approach that places student learning at its centre. It focuses on how students learn, not just on what they learn. We, as teachers, need to encourage learners to 'think hard', rather than passively receive information. Active learning encourages learners to take responsibility for their learning and supports them in becoming independent and confident learners in school and beyond.

Assessment for Learning

Assessment for Learning (AfL) is a teaching approach that generates feedback which can be used to improve learners' performance. Learners become more involved in the learning process and, from this, gain confidence in what they are expected to learn and to what standard. We, as teachers, gain insights into a learner's level of understanding of a particular concept or topic, which helps to inform how we support their progression.

Differentiation

Differentiation is usually presented as a teaching approach where teachers think of learners as individuals and learning as a personalised process. Whilst precise definitions can vary, typically the core aim of differentiation is viewed as ensuring that all learners, no matter their ability, interest or context, make progress towards their learning intentions. It is about using different approaches and appreciating the differences in learners to help them make progress. Teachers therefore need to be responsive, and willing and able to adapt their teaching to meet the needs of their learners.

Language awareness

For many learners, English is an additional language. It might be their second or perhaps their third language. Depending on the school context, students might be learning all or just some of their subjects through English.

For all learners, regardless of whether they are learning through their first language or an additional language, language is a vehicle for learning. It is through language that students access the learning intentions of the lesson and communicate their ideas. It is our responsibility, as teachers, to ensure that language doesn't present a barrier to learning.

Metacognition

Metacognition describes the processes involved when learners plan, monitor, evaluate and make changes to their own learning behaviours. These processes help learners to think about their own learning more explicitly and ensure that they are able to meet a learning goal that they have identified themselves or that we, as teachers, have set.

Skills for Life

How do we prepare learners to succeed in a fast-changing world? To collaborate with people from around the globe? To create innovation as technology increasingly takes over routine work? To use advanced thinking skills in the face of more complex challenges? To show resilience in the face of constant change? At Cambridge, we are responding to educators who have asked for a way to understand how all these different approaches to life skills and competencies relate to their teaching. We have grouped these skills into six main Areas of Competency that can be incorporated into teaching, and have examined the different stages of the learning journey and how these competencies vary across each stage.

These six key areas are:
- Creativity – finding new ways of doing things, and solutions to problems
- Collaboration – the ability to work well with others
- Communication – speaking and presenting confidently and participating effectively in meetings
- Critical thinking – evaluating what is heard or read, and linking ideas constructively
- Learning to learn – developing the skills to learn more effectively
- Social responsibilities – contributing to social groups, and being able to talk to and work with people from other cultures.

Cambridge learner and teacher attributes

This course helps develop the following Cambridge learner and teacher attributes.

Cambridge learners	Cambridge teachers
Confident in working with information and ideas – their own and those of others.	Confident in teaching their subject and engaging each student in learning.
Responsible for themselves, responsive to and respectful of others.	Responsible for themselves, responsive to and respectful of others.
Reflective as learners, developing their ability to learn.	Reflective as learners themselves, developing their practice.
Innovative and equipped for new and future challenges.	Innovative and equipped for new and future challenges.
Engaged intellectually and socially, ready to make a difference.	Engaged intellectually, professionally and socially, ready to make a difference.

Reproduced from Developing the Cambridge learner attributes *with permission from Cambridge Assessment International Education.*

⬇ More information about these approaches to learning and teaching is available to download from Cambridge GO (as part of this Teacher's Resource).

> Research

SKILLS SECTION	CROSS-CURRICULAR LINKS *Learners have opportunities to apply their knowledge and understanding of, and skills in:*	TOPICS MODELLED
Starting with	**Geography: human geography** • Understanding human characteristics of places **Language skills: speaking and listening** • Listen, reflect on what is heard and give a reasoned response with reference to at least one specific point made by the speaker **Maths: statistics** • Record, organise and represent categorical, discrete and continuous data • Choose and explain which representation to use in a given situation **Science: thinking and working scientifically** • Describe the accuracy of predictions based on results • Present and interpret results using tables, bar charts, dot plots, line graphs and scatter graphs	Moving goods and people Reduce, re-use, recycle
Developing	**Language skills: reading** • Explore explicit meanings in a range of texts • Explore implicit meanings in a range of texts **Language skills: speaking and listening** • Use language to convey ideas and opinions, with increasing clarity and detail **Maths: statistics** • Record, organise and represent categorical, discrete and continuous data • Choose and explain which representation to use in a given situation **Science: thinking and working scientifically** • Describe the accuracy of predictions based on results • Present and interpret results using tables, bar charts, dot plots, line graphs and scatter graphs	Sharing Planet Earth Moving goods and people
Getting better at	**Science: thinking and working scientifically** • Sort, group and classify objects, materials and living things through testing, observation and using secondary information • Describe the accuracy of predictions, based on results • Use a range of secondary information sources to research and select relevant evidence to answer questions • Collect and record observations and/or measurements in tables and diagrams appropriate to the type of scientific enquiry	Keeping healthy Moving goods and people

SKILLS SECTION	CROSS-CURRICULAR LINKS *Learners have opportunities to apply their knowledge and understanding of, and skills in:*	TOPICS MODELLED
	Maths: statistics • Plan and conduct an investigation, and make predictions for a set of related statistical questions, considering what data to collect • Record, organise and represent categorical, discrete and continuous data • Choose and explain which representation to use in a given situation Geography: human geography • Finding different solutions to environmental issues	

The cross-curricular links in this table are reproduced from Cambridge International curriculum frameworks. This Cambridge International copyright material is reproduced under licence and remains the intellectual property of Cambridge Assessment International Education.

Starting with research skills: Lesson 1

In Lesson 1, learners focus on starting to construct research questions, by considering what is meant by 'global issues' and identifying different types of question, and by starting to make their own questions about such issues.

CAMBRIDGE STAGE 6 RESEARCH LEARNING OBJECTIVES

1.1 Constructing research questions: Begin to construct research questions with support

LESSON LEARNING GOALS

To start to:
• say what a global issue is
• identify different types of question
• make my own questions to help me understand global issues.

Resources needed

Learner's Skills Book 6

Downloadables 1.1 and 1.2

Challenge topic (e.g. Moving goods and people, Reduce, re-use, recycle)

Prior learning (approx. 5–10 mins)

Good for: Building on previous knowledge.

Activity: Ask learners to discuss what 'global issues' means.

Ways of working: Give learners time to discuss global issues in pairs or small groups before staging a plenary session in which learners share and respond to each other's ideas.

Differentiation: Support learners by showing pictures of global issues and asking them to identify what the issue is from the picture. Challenge learners to come up with their own examples of global issues and to rank global issues according to which they see as being the most important.

Suggested answers: Look for and encourage responses that acknowledge 'global issues' as those which affect a large number of people around the world (e.g. technological developments, such as humans being replaced by machines in the workplace) or which impact on the planet itself (e.g. deforestation, pollution, climate change). Contrast these with issues that are specific to the learners' local community (although these too may have a global dimension).

Starter activity (approx. 10–15 mins)

Good for: Starting to understand the difference between local and global issues, and how they may be inter-related; identifying different types of questions that can be asked about an issue.

Activity: Read through the learning goals for this lesson with learners at the beginning of this activity. After looking at an example, ask learners to identify another local issue that has global dimensions and complete a table by listing some of the problems it causes.

Ways of working: Learners work in pairs or small groups to complete the table. In a plenary session, encourage learners to share and respond to each other's ideas.

Differentiation: Support learners by checking their understanding of the example based on transport by using questioning. Continuing with the issue of transport, they can then consider how it affects them personally in order to complete the table. Challenge learners to come up with another global issue that has local consequences and complete the table using their answers.

Suggested answers: Look for and encourage responses that clearly identify a local issue with global dimensions. Encourage learners to talk about their personal experiences of any such issues.

Main activity (approx. 20–25 mins)

Good for: Helping learners to start identifying different types of question that can be asked about an issue and making up their own questions to develop a deeper understanding of it.

Activity: After looking at an example of how a mind-map can be used to generate questions about an issue, ask learners to identify different types of question as local, national or global. Then ask them to choose a different topic and make up their own questions about it, following this model.

Ways of working: Learners work in pairs or small groups to identify different types of question in the table. Check their answers in a plenary session using the Worked Example in Downloadable 1.1.

Learners then work in pairs or small groups to come up with a different topic and write their own questions to complete another table (a template is provided as Downloadable 1.2). Follow this with a plenary session, encouraging learners to share and respond to each other's ideas. (If time allows, ask each pair or group to read out one of their questions, getting others to identify whether it is a local, national or global question.)

Differentiation: Support learners by checking their understanding of the questions in the mind-map by using questioning. Give them a topic of local interest to focus on, and encourage them to come up with one example of each type of question (local, national and global). Challenge learners to come up with their own topic and to identify a number of local, national and global questions about it.

Suggested answers: See the Worked Example for Zara's table in Downloadable 1.1.

Starting with research skills: Lesson 2

In Lesson 2, learners focus on starting to develop information skills, by identifying different types of source relevant to a topic; conducting research, by designing questionnaires to use in an investigation and making simple predictions about the outcome of an investigation; and recording findings, by choosing an appropriate method of selecting, organising and recording research findings.

CAMBRIDGE STAGE 6 RESEARCH LEARNING OBJECTIVES

1.2 Information skills: Identify sources and locate relevant information and answers to questions within them

1.3 Conducting research: Conduct investigations, using interviews or questionnaires to test a prediction or begin to answer a research question

1.4 Recording findings: Select, organise and record relevant information from sources and findings from research using an appropriate method

LESSON LEARNING GOALS

To start to:

- recognise different types of sources that can help me to find out about a topic
- design a questionnaire to use in an investigation
- make simple predictions about what I think I will find out in an investigation
- choose a suitable way of selecting, organising and recording what I find out.

Resources needed

Learner's Skills Book 6

Downloadable 1.3

Challenge topic (e.g. Moving goods and people, Reduce, re-use, recycle)

Prior learning (approx. 5–10 mins)

Good for: Building on previous knowledge.

Activity: Ask learners to identify questions about local, national and global issues.

Ways of working: Give learners time to discuss and compare their answers in pairs or small groups before staging a plenary session in which a whole-class check can be carried out.

Differentiation: Support learners by asking them first to identify the question that refers to a local issue by using questioning to check their understanding of each question. Challenge learners to explain how they decided whether a question was global, national or local.

Suggested answers: 1 = national question; 2 = global question; 3 = local question.

Starter activity (approx. 10–15 mins)

Good for: Starting to think about different sources that could be used to find out about a topic and how sources about local issues might be different from sources for national or global issues.

Activity: Read through the learning goals for this lesson with learners at the beginning of this activity. Ask learners to consider what sources might be useful to investigate each question and to decide the one they think the best.

Ways of working: Learners can work individually at first. They then share their ideas in pairs or small groups in order to complete each of the statements beginning 'The best way to find out would be . . . ' In a plenary session, encourage learners to share and respond to each other's ideas.

Differentiation: Support learners by checking their understanding of questions 1–3 using questioning. Ask them to focus on the question referring to a local issue and think of ways they could find out more about it. Challenge learners to come up with a variety of different sources for each question and to explain which they think is the best.

Suggested answers: Although it isn't necessary for the learners to know the terms 'primary research' and 'secondary research', look for an understanding that, in order to answer the first two questions, the learners could gather data directly themselves, for example by interviewing people, using questionnaires, to carry out a survey. For the third question, they are much more likely to suggest accessing data produced by other people's research, and that is available online or in books, newspapers, magazines, and so on.

For the class discussion, get feedback from pairs or groups on which sources they think would be most useful for each question and allow discussion of any differences of opinion that might arise. There is no need to insist on a 'right' or 'wrong' answer, so long as learners can justify the choice they have made.

Main activity (approx. 20–25 mins)

Good for: Starting to think about ways of designing questionnaires to make selecting, organising and recording research findings more efficient, and for making simple predictions about the outcome of an investigation.

Activity: Ask learners to look at two methods of organising research findings, deciding which is the more efficient. They apply what they have learnt in order to design their own questionnaire and make a simple prediction about what they will find out.

Ways of working: Learners work in pairs or small groups to discuss the two different methods of organising research findings before sharing their ideas and responding to others in a plenary session. They continue to work in pairs or small groups to design their own questionnaire (a template is provided in Downloadable 1.3) and make a simple prediction.

Differentiation: Support learners by checking their understanding of the questionnaire and making a tally to record results using questioning (e.g. 'What is this questionnaire about?', 'What question did they ask?', 'How did they record people's answers?', etc.). Challenge learners to work independently or in pairs or groups to design their own questionnaire on a topic of their choice and make predictions.

Suggested answers: The first example showing how answers to the question 'How do you travel to school?' have been recorded is deliberately designed to show learners an inefficient way of doing this, and is not intended as a model for them to follow. Encourage learners to point out some of the problems with this way of recording data – for example, it's confusing because it lacks organisation, consists of a mixture of text and numerical data, lacks consistent categories or headings, contains a lot of

irrelevant information (e.g. names), is unclear (how many 'friends' come with Ken in his dad's car?), and so on.

The tally chart has a number of advantages (e.g. use of headings, clear method of recording data in a tally, all data expressed as numbers, etc.). Check also that learners understand that the 'Other' heading is a way of dealing with answers that they have not predicted.

Peer feedback (approx. 5–10 mins)

Pair each learner with a partner from a different group. Ask them to think about features of each other's questionnaires, such as their choice of topic, how clear the question is, whether they have predicted the most likely answers to their question, and so on.

Starting with research skills: Lesson 3

In Lesson 3, learners focus on starting to develop information skills, by finding information in sources to answer questions; conducting research, by thinking of questions to ask when interviewing someone; and recording findings, by recognising different ways of selecting, organising and recording information from sources.

CAMBRIDGE STAGE 6 RESEARCH LEARNING OBJECTIVES

1.2 Information skills: Identify sources and locate relevant information and answers to questions within them

1.3 Conducting research: Conduct investigations, using interviews or questionnaires to test a prediction or begin to answer a research question

1.4 Recording findings: Select, organise and record relevant information from sources and findings from research using an appropriate method

LESSON LEARNING GOALS

To start to:

- find information in sources to answer my own questions

- think of my own questions to ask when interviewing someone

- recognise different ways of selecting, organising and recording information from sources.

Resources needed

Learner's Skills Book 6

Downloadable 1.4

Challenge topic (e.g. Moving goods and people, Reduce, re-use, recycle)

Prior learning (approx. 5–10 mins)

Good for: Building on previous knowledge.

Activity: Ask learners to recall what they already know about predictions and to make their own predictions on the topics given.

Ways of working: Learners can work individually, making their own predictions before sharing them with others in pairs or small groups. Stage a plenary session, encouraging learners to share and respond to each other's ideas.

Differentiation: Support learners by checking their understanding of the topics they are to make predictions about by using questioning. Challenge learners to explain the predictions they have made (e.g. by describing what information or knowledge was useful to them).

Suggested answers: Accept any reasonable predictions, especially where learners can give reasons to support their ideas.

Starter activity (approx. 10–15 mins)

Good for: Starting to plan an investigation by making decisions about what sources to use, what questions to ask and how to organise research findings.

Activity: Read through the learning goals for this lesson with learners at the beginning of this activity. Ask learners to discuss the topic of lateness among learners arriving at school in the morning and consider how to investigate it.

Ways of working: Give learners the opportunity to work in pairs or small groups to discuss the questions before holding a class discussion. Encourage learners to share and respond to each other's ideas.

Differentiation: Support learners by checking their understanding of the discussion topic by using questioning. Encourage learners to speak about their own personal experience of the topic. Challenge learners to explain the possible reasons for lateness and consider how they could be investigated.

Suggested answers: Accept any reasonable responses, especially where learners can offer reasons or evidence for their ideas. Encourage learners to draw on what they have learnt in the previous lesson, reminding them of the distinction between 'primary' and 'secondary' sources and highlighting the importance of the former in an investigation of this type.

Main activity (approx. 15–20 mins)

Good for: Starting to think of what questions to ask when carrying out an interview in order to elicit relevant information, and of how to record responses to the questions.

Activity: Ask learners to look at the questionnaire form and come up with appropriate questions to ask in order to elicit all the relevant information. Learners then complete the questionnaire by using their questions to interview a partner, and recording their partner's responses.

Ways of working: Learners can work individually at first to come up with appropriate questions, then in pairs or small groups to decide which questions would be most appropriate and efficient at eliciting the relevant information. Pair learners so that they can conduct interviews using the questionnaire. Encourage learners to use polite forms of address when carrying out their interviews (e.g. 'Would you mind if I ask you some questions?', 'Thank you for your time', etc.). Having used the questionnaire to interview a partner, learners can then report back to the class in a plenary session, sharing their experience of conducting an interview and discussing how this method of research might be improved.

Differentiation: Support learners by checking their understanding of the questionnaire format by using questioning. Challenge learners by asking them to refine their questions to find the most efficient way of eliciting the relevant information in an interview.

Suggested answers: There can be some variety in the form the questions take, but learners should be encouraged to elicit the relevant information in the most efficient way – for example, by asking one question, such as 'How do you travel to school?' rather than by asking 'Do you come by car? Do you come by bus?' and so on.

The following questions could be asked:

1   How do you travel to school?

2   How long does it take?

3   Who travels to school with you?

4   How often are you late?

5   Why are you late?

Answers to the first four questions can be recorded with a tick in the appropriate box, but the fifth question requires a written response.

For a Worked Example of a completed questionnaire, see Downloadable 1.4.

Taking it further: Lessons 1–3

How do your learners travel to school? Based on their work in Lesson 2, encourage learners to think of the pros and cons of each method of travel that is used by their classmates. Stage a debate, with learners arguing in favour of their preferred method of travel, pointing out its advantages and the disadvantages of other methods.

What have your learners discovered about the reasons for lateness among their peers in Lesson 3? Encourage them to work in groups to present their findings in creative ways, for instance by producing a poster ('Don't be late!') offering advice on how to avoid lateness.

Alternatively, they could script a short dramatic sketch (e.g. a dialogue between a teacher and a learner arriving late to class) to put their message across and present this in a class assembly.

Developing research skills: Lesson 4

In Lesson 4, learners focus on developing information skills, by clarifying the difference between ways of carrying out research and ways of recording results; and constructing research questions, by investigating which of two contrasting perspectives is most supported by evidence.

CAMBRIDGE STAGE 6 RESEARCH LEARNING OBJECTIVES

1.1 Constructing research questions: Begin to construct research questions with support

1.2 Information skills: Identify sources and locate relevant information and answers to questions within them

LESSON LEARNING GOALS

To develop my knowledge and understanding about:

- making questions that help me investigate a topic
- deciding what sources will help me find out more about a topic.

Resources needed

Learner's Skills Book 6

Challenge topic (e.g. Sharing Planet Earth, Moving goods and people)

Optional:

Books from other subjects where learners have recorded results, for example science (experiments), geography (field trips)

Extracts from a local newspaper, textbooks in the school library

Extracts from the school's website or blog, and so on

Prior learning (approx. 5 mins)

Good for: Building on previous knowledge.

Activity: Learners sort ideas into a table: 'ways of carrying out research' and 'ways of recording results'.

Ways of working: Give learners time to consider this individually before discussing with a partner. Books from other subjects where learners have carried out research of any kind could be used for ideas.

Differentiation: Support learners who are unsure, by discussing further examples from the table in 'suggested answers' below with reference to books from other subjects where learners have recorded results, for example science (experiments), geography (field trips). Challenge learners to provide further examples, especially of carrying out 'first-hand' or 'primary' research.

Suggested answers:

Ways of carrying out research	Ways of recording results
• interviewing people • making a prediction • reading articles online • using a questionnaire	• making a graph or chart • making a table • making a tally chart • taking notes

Starter activity (approx. 10 mins)

Good for: Learners to consider where they stand with regard to two contrasting perspectives on litter.

Activity: Read through the learning goals for this lesson with learners at the beginning of this activity. Learners decide if they agree with Marcus's perspective (children in their school litter because they think it is normal) or Sofia's (there are not enough bins).

Ways of working: You could take a preliminary vote, for example point to the window if you agree with Marcus, point to the door if you agree with Sofia, point to the ceiling if you are unsure. Try to stimulate discussion by asking learners to talk to someone who has a different view.

Differentiation: Support learners by encouraging them to draw on their own experiences. Have they seen litter (if only on TV)? Where? What do they think caused it? Challenge learners to justify whether they agree with Marcus or Sofia (or both). On what basis do they make their judgement? Are alternative explanations possible? Is better infrastructure always the solution to a problem? Is taking personal responsibility always enough?

Suggested answers: The best responses will use their prior experience to make a general point, for example 'I agree with Sofia, because the children I know say they do care but they might both be wrong. It doesn't matter how much you care about litter or how many bins there are if the bins are all put in a windy place.' Or 'I agree with Marcus, because people are more likely to respect places that are neat and tidy in the first place.'

Main activity (approx. 20–25 mins)

Good for: Learners to consider what sources and questions would help them decide whose perspective makes most sense.

Activity: Learners rank a selection of sources according to how useful they would be to decide on the cause of the litter problem. They then decide what questions they would need to ask.

Ways of working: You could have learners working individually on both parts of the activity prior to the class discussion. Alternatively, you could come to a class agreement first about which sources would be most useful and then discuss what questions they could best help address.

Differentiation: Support learners by showing them some of the suggested resources and ask them questions. For example, show a local newspaper; does it look like it would cover stories like litter in the playground? If not, this can be ranked lower than another source that does address the topic. Challenge learners by asking them to consider what useful different perspectives could be obtained from a range of sources. Support learners by giving some initial ideas from the suggestions below – they can then follow a 'who, what, where, when, why, how' structure. Challenge them to focus their questions, targeting particular sources.

Suggested answers:

1 A possible ranking order, with reasons, might be:

   1 Other children at their school – are most likely to have direct experience of the problem.

   2 Teachers and parents of children at their school – will have experience over time of the issue.

   3 The school's website and blog – could record appeals in the past for tidiness.

   4 Textbooks in the school library – might contain information on looking after the environment in general.

   5 Articles in the local newspaper – could possibly contain a success story (but very unlikely).

   6 Documentaries on local TV – litter in the playground would likely be quite low on the producers' priorities.

2 Suggested questions include:

   • Who thinks that the litter in the playground is normal?

   • Where is the problem worst?

   • How have people tried to deal with the problem in other places?

- When is the problem worst?
- Why do people drop litter?
- What has been done before to try and deal with the problem?

For the class discussion question 'What other actions could they take to get a full understanding of the problem?', possible answers might be:

- interview children
- compile a questionnaire
- conduct a survey to find out more precisely when the problem happens
- contact children in different schools to find out whether they have the same problem and if not, what they do about it.

Developing research skills: Lesson 5

In Lesson 5, learners focus on developing information skills, by using the findings of a survey and locating information in this source to answer questions. They are introduced to different ways in which findings that have been recorded can be used as part of conducting research.

CAMBRIDGE STAGE 6 RESEARCH LEARNING OBJECTIVES

1.2 Information skills: Identify sources and locate relevant information and answers to questions within them

1.3 Conducting research: Conduct investigations, using interviews or questionnaires to test a prediction or begin to answer a research question

1.4 Recording findings: Select, organise and record relevant information from sources and findings from research using an appropriate method

LESSON LEARNING GOALS

To develop my knowledge and understanding about:

- reading a tally chart
- using the results of a questionnaire
- looking at results and using them to suggest a course of action.

Resources needed

Learner's Skills Book 6 – this includes Sofia and Marcus's results

Downloadables 1.5, 1.6 and 1.7

Challenge topic (e.g. Sharing Planet Earth, Moving goods and people)

Prior learning (approx. 5 mins)

Good for: Activating prior understanding of the issue (litter) and different perspectives on its causes.

Activity: Class discussion of Sofia and Marcus's perspectives in the previous lesson – who do they agree with and why?

Ways of working: You could employ the 'quick vote' technique used in Lesson 4. Alternatively, learners could be given a set amount of time to consider their decision before you select individuals to feed back to the class. Others could be asked if they share the view that has just been expressed.

Differentiation: Support learners by encouraging them to look back and use the way Sofia and Marcus back up their opinions. Challenge learners to apply again their own understanding of the issue based on their experience. Is it an issue as far as they are concerned? What, in their view, is/are the main cause(s)? Have they any experience of a different approach to the problem?

Suggested answers:

1 Litter in the playground.

2 The lack of bins was the main cause.

3 Litter is so common that children think it is normal.

4 The character who learners agree with most will depend on their experience of the issue. A wide range of answers are possible – for example, 'Marcus is right; around my area, it is so messy that people never bother with bins.' or 'Sofia is right; I know our playground bin overflows easily.'

Starter activity (approx. 5 mins)

Good for: Starting out with facts before making inferences from a set of data.

Activity: Read through the learning goals for this lesson with learners at the beginning of this activity. Learners are asked what we know for sure from these results.

Ways of working: A good way of a conducting whole-class assessment for learning would be to give a statement and ask, for example, 'Point to the window if you think we can be confident this statement is true; point to the door if you think we can't', and so on.

Differentiation: Support learners by encouraging them to use the data and state facts (e.g. 'Only one child surveyed disagreed with the statement, 'there is too much litter on the playground'). Challenge learners to use expressions of degree appropriately (e.g. 'The overwhelming majority believes that . . . ', 'A significant proportion think that . . . ').

Suggested answers:

Only one person disagreed with the statement 'There is too much litter on the school playground at break time.'

The vast majority agreed with the statement 'There is too much litter on the school playground at break time.'

A significant majority disagreed with the statement 'Children drop litter because they do not care about the environment.'

Only one person thought that there were enough litter bins on the playground for everyone's rubbish.

Main activity (approx. 30 mins)

Good for: Learners to use data and understand that conclusions can be drawn with varying degrees of certainty. It is OK to infer what data is telling us as long as we understand that is what we're doing.

Activity: Learners read statements based on questionnaire data and decide the best descriptions: 'certainly true'; 'likely to be true'; 'cannot be sure'; 'likely to be false'; 'certainly false'.

Ways of working: This would lend itself well to pair work with partners taking turns to give their opinion first before recording. If using the differentiation activity in Downloadable 1.6 (see Differentiation below), support learners by encouraging them to work with their partner to rule out the options that have least basis in the results first. Challenge learners to discuss with their partner the likely outcomes of each option based on their own experiences, the results and their perspective.

Differentiation: Support learners by working through more of the suggested answers (see Downloadable 1.5) with them. Challenge learners to suggest other possible statements that fit each of the criteria. Challenge learners further by using the activity in Downloadable 1.6, in which learners are asked to select the best action that Marcus and Sofia could take to solve the problem of litter on the playground.

Suggested answers: Downloadable 1.5 provides a Worked Example to the Main activity. See Downloadable 1.7 for a Worked Example for the differentiation activity.

Peer feedback (approx. 5 mins)

Pair each learner with a partner from a different group. Ask them to give feedback on whether the decisions 'certainly true'; 'likely to be true'; 'cannot be sure'; 'likely to be false'; 'certainly false' are supported by the results.

Alternatively, if you have used Downloadable 1.6, pair each learner with a partner from a different group. Ask them to give feedback on whether their proposed solution is in fact supported by the results.

Developing research skills: Lesson 6

In Lesson 6, learners focus on developing their skills in conducting an investigation about an issue, by devising statements that can be used to help test a prediction. They record relevant information and use it to summarise what people think about the problem they are investigating.

CAMBRIDGE STAGE 6 RESEARCH LEARNING OBJECTIVES

1.3 Conducting research: Conduct investigations, using interviews or questionnaires to test a prediction or begin to answer a research question

1.4 Recording findings: Select, organise and record relevant information from sources and findings from research using an appropriate method

LESSON LEARNING GOALS

To develop my knowledge and understanding about:

- how to conduct a survey and record my findings using a tally chart
- how to interpret the results of a questionnaire
- how to look at results and use them to see if my prediction was accurate.

Resources needed

Learner's Skills Book 6

Downloadable 1.8

Challenge topic (e.g. Sharing Planet Earth, Moving goods and people)

Mini-whiteboards (if available)

Prior learning (approx. 5 mins)

Good for: Activating prior understanding. Re-orientating learners to a global issue that has a local impact.

Activity: Learners are asked to look back to Lesson 1 of this unit and give the name of a global issue that matters in their home area. They are prompted to recall some of the problems it causes.

Ways of working: This would lend itself well to a 'think/pair/share' approach. Learners could show their responses on mini-whiteboards to aid Assessment for Learning.

Differentiation: Support learners by recapping the names (and local impacts) of global issues. Challenge learners to deepen their explanation by exploring how different groups of people are impacted in different ways.

Suggested answers: Refer back to Lesson 1.

Starter activity (approx. 10 mins)

Good for: Applying the understanding of local issues developed earlier in the unit and using this to devise statements that can be used in to conduct research.

Activity: Read through the learning goals for this lesson with learners at the beginning of this activity. Learners discuss the local problem and why they think the problem is happening. They list some possible reasons.

Ways of working: This section of the lesson could be divided into discussion time and quiet focused time to record ideas.

Differentiation: Support learners by discussing Worked Examples. Challenge learners to deepen their explanation by exploring a range of long- / short-term causes.

Suggested answers:

For a topic on litter:

The problem: There's a problem with children dropping litter on the playground during break time.

Possible reasons: Children drop litter because they don't care about the environment. They're so used to seeing litter on the streets, they think it's perfectly normal. There's only one litter bin. It gets filled up very quickly and then there's nowhere to put litter. The bin is the wrong design.

For a topic on transport:

The problem: The traffic in our area is really bad, so children are late to school.

Possible reasons: People use the street by our school as a short cut. There aren't enough buses and they're too expensive. People drive to drop their children off when they could walk.

Main activity (approx. 30 mins)

Good for: Practical experience of devising a questionnaire, using it to conduct a survey and interpreting the results.

Activity: Learners carry out an investigation to find out what other people think about their issue. They first make some predictions about what they think the results will be. They make three statements and then ask others to agree or disagree with them in order to check their predictions.

Ways of working: The people that are surveyed will need to be those who are affected by the issue being considered. If this is to be conducted outside class with members of the community, then appropriate safeguarding policies will need to be adhered to. The survey could be conducted in the lesson with members of the class. If this is the case, then care will need to be given to ensure that the issue under consideration is something about which the learners are able to express an opinion through personal experience.

Differentiation: Support learners by discussing the suggested answers. Challenge learners to deepen their explanation of what they have found out by exploring what impact their findings have on possible solutions to the problem. Challenge them further to consider how different groups of people are impacted in different ways by the problem, for example younger children, older children, adults, the elderly, disabled people, parents with babies.

Suggested answers:

For litter as the topic:

Problem: There's a problem with children dropping litter on the playground during break time.

Prediction: I think most children don't notice the litter and don't care.

Statements: There's too much litter on the school playground at break time. Children drop litter because they don't care about the environment. There aren't enough litter bins on the playground for everyone's rubbish.

For transport as the topic:

Problem: The traffic in our area is really bad, so children are late to school.

Predictions: Children don't like it when people use the street by our school as a short cut. Children do not like going on the bus. More children could walk.

Statements: The street by our school is too busy because people use it as a short cut. Children do not like going on the bus. More children could walk.

For a Worked Example showing how a completed survey on transport might look, see Downloadable 1.8.

Suggested answers:

For the reflection questions using the transport topic:

1   Children think that too many people use the street by our school as a short cut. It is not true that children do not like going on the bus. It is not clear if children could walk.

2   Children think that too many people use the street by our school as a short cut. I think that they don't like it, but I can't prove that – I didn't ask them.

3   Bar charts, pie charts.

Taking it further: Lessons 4–6

In response to Sofia's and Marcus's perspectives in the Starter activity in Lesson 4, challenge learners to develop their exchange in the Learner's Skills Book into a dialogue. How would they justify their perspective? How would the other person respond?

This could be set up as a role play in the first instance and could also be developed as a written dialogue as a play script or following narrative conventions.

Taking the tally chart in Lesson 5 as a starting point, challenge learners to handle their data in more sophisticated ways by constructing and reading pictograms with whole and part pictures. Understanding the idea that we can make conclusions to varying degrees of certainty could be reinforced in other subjects, for example science, by exploring the use of statements such as 'Is certainly true', 'Is likely to be true', 'We cannot be sure', 'Is likely to be false', 'Is certainly false'.

Learners could benefit from a different local or indeed international comparative perspective by corresponding with learners in a partner school. How does the global issue you identified have an impact in their area? What problems do they experience? Have they experience of any effective solutions?

Getting better at research skills: Lesson 7

In Lesson 7, learners focus on getting better at conducting research, by deciding if a prediction is correct according to the results of an investigation; and on recording findings, by considering the advantages of one way of presenting the results of an investigation.

CAMBRIDGE STAGE 6 RESEARCH LEARNING OBJECTIVES

1.3 Conducting research: Conduct investigations, using interviews or questionnaires to test a prediction or begin to answer a research question

1.4 Recording findings: Select, organise and record relevant information from sources and findings from research using an appropriate method

LESSON LEARNING GOALS

To get better at:

- deciding whether a prediction is correct as a result of carrying out an investigation

- giving reasons for choosing a way of way of selecting, organising and recording information from a source.

Resources needed

Learner's Skills Book 6

Downloadable 1.9

Challenge topic (e.g. Keeping healthy, Moving goods and people)

Prior learning (approx. 5–10 mins)

Good for: Building on previous knowledge.

Activity: Ask learners to identify from a list which statements are predictions.

Ways of working: Learners work individually at first, then in pairs or small groups to discuss their answers. Stage a plenary session to check answers with the whole class.

Differentiation: Support learners by checking their understanding of the term 'prediction' by using questioning and giving examples before asking them to complete the activity. Challenge learners to give reasons for their answers.

Suggested answers: For a Worked Example of the table, see Downloadable 1.9. Statements 1, 3 and 4 are predictions because they are statements about the future where the outcome is uncertain.

Starter activity (approx. 10–15 mins)

Good for: Focusing learners' attention on the local consequences of a global issue and thinking about how the local situation can be improved.

Activity: Read through the learning goals for this lesson with learners at the beginning of this activity. Ask learners to read the short texts and engage in a class discussion about the local consequences of a global issue.

Ways of working: Give learners the opportunity to work in pairs or small groups to discuss the questions before staging a plenary session. In the plenary, encourage groups to share their ideas and respond to others.

Differentiation: Support learners by checking their understanding of the short texts by using questioning and focusing on any vocabulary that is likely to cause difficulty. Challenge learners to come up with a variety of responses to each question, giving evidence and reasoning where appropriate.

Suggested answers: Accept any reasonable responses, especially if supported by evidence or reasoning. Encourage learners to draw on their own personal experiences, to express different opinions about the issue and to consider other people's perspectives.

Main activity (approx. 15–20 mins)

Good for: Understanding the decision-making process when planning an investigation, especially with regard to organising the collection and presentation of data, and then using the data to check whether a prediction is correct.

Activity: Ask learners to read some background information about an investigation; learners then look at how data has been collected and presented and decide whether a prediction is correct.

Ways of working: Learners work in pairs or small groups to discuss the investigation, the way the findings are presented and whether or not the prediction is correct before engaging in a whole-class discussion of these topics.

Differentiation: Support learners by checking their understanding of the questionnaire and the bar chart by using questioning. Challenge learners to say what the data in the bar chart means and to comment critically on the questionnaire and the bar chart as ways of collecting and presenting data.

Suggested answers: Accept any reasonable responses, especially those supported by evidence or reasoning. Check that learners understand how the questionnaire

is structured, so that if an interviewee responds 'Yes' to the first question, there is no need to ask the follow-up questions; similarly, Question 3 is only asked if the interviewee chooses B for Question 2. This is an example of using a sequence of connected questions to structure a questionnaire.

The prediction is correct, because a majority of the interviewees were in favour of changing the system to having a drink with them at all times, even if this could only be water. Bar charts provide a clear graphic presentation of these results, which could be used to persuade others that changes are needed, possibly by including them in posters or as part of a presentation delivered in a school assembly.

Getting better at research skills: Lesson 8

In Lesson 8, learners focus on getting better at constructing research questions, by thinking about the local consequences of global issues and what questions can be asked about them; and on information skills, by considering what sources they could use to find the answers to their questions.

CAMBRIDGE STAGE 6 RESEARCH LEARNING OBJECTIVES

1.1 Constructing research questions: Begin to construct research questions with support

1.2 Information skills: Identify sources and locate relevant information and answers to questions within them

LESSON LEARNING GOALS

To get better at:

- understanding what makes a global and local issue
- making my own questions in order to understand global and local issues
- identifying useful sources for finding answers to my questions.

Resources needed

Learner's Skills Book 6

Downloadables 1.10, 1.11 and 1.12

Challenge topic (e.g. Keeping healthy, Moving goods and people)

Causes and consequences in Starter activity printed onto slips of paper, if needed

Examples of sources that can be used to find out more about local issues (see Starter activity)

Prior learning (approx. 5–10 mins)

Good for: Building on previous knowledge.

Activity: Ask learners to discuss what they know about global issues and their local impacts.

Ways of working: Learners work in pairs or small groups to discuss the questions. Stage a plenary session, encouraging learners to share and respond to each other's ideas.

Differentiation: Support learners by checking their understanding of the terms 'global issue' and 'local impact' by using questioning and giving examples of each. Challenge learners to come up with their own examples of global issues and their local impacts.

Suggested answers: Accept any reasonable responses, especially where learners can provide evidence or reasoning to support their ideas.

Starter activity (approx. 10–15 mins)

Good for: Focusing learners' attention on a number of global issues, their causes and consequence, which can then be linked to local impacts.

Activity: Read through the learning goals for this lesson with learners at the beginning of this activity. Ask learners to sort and match causes and consequences of global issues.

Ways of working: Learners can work individually at first, then in pairs or small groups to share their ideas. Examples of sources can be used to find out more about local issues. Stage a plenary session to check the activity with the whole class.

Differentiation: Support learners by checking their understanding of the terms 'cause' and 'consequence' by using questioning and giving examples. Give additional support by providing copies of each of the causes and consequences printed out on separate slips of paper so that they can be physically sorted and matched. If preferred, sort the causes and consequences into sets first, so that the learners' task is to match causes and consequences. Challenge learners to come up with additional causes and consequences related to global issues (e.g. plastic pollution, education for all, etc.).

Suggested answers: See the Worked Example in Downloadable 1.10. For the class discussion, accept any reasonable responses, especially if supported by evidence or reasoning. Encourage learners to express different opinions about local consequences and the actions being taken to deal with them, and to consider other people's perspectives on these issues. Be prepared to provide learners with information about sources they could use to inform themselves about local consequences (e.g. secondary sources such as local newspapers – in print and online – local radio and television, authorities or institutions such as the local council, libraries, etc.; and primary sources such as people living or working in the local community who could be interviewed, etc.).

Main activity (approx. 15–20 mins)

Good for: Thinking about what questions to ask when investigating a local issue and what sources could be used to find the answers.

Activity: Ask learners to look at an example of how a mind-map can be used to generate ideas and questions about a local issue; learners can then create a mind-map of their own (see the template in Downloadable 1.11 and the Worked Example in Downloadable 1.12) based on an issue of local interest.

Ways of working: Learners work in pairs or small groups to create their own mind-maps focusing on a local issue. When this process is complete, ask each group to report to the whole class on what questions they have come up with and what sources they could use to find answers to the questions. Give learners the opportunity to respond to others' ideas.

Differentiation: Support learners by checking their understanding of the mind-map and what it shows by using questioning. Give additional support by identifying an issue with local relevance for learners to focus on, encouraging them to share their personal experiences of the issue. Challenge learners by asking them to identify an issue of local relevance and to come up with their own questions to ask about it, with ideas about what sources they could use to find answers to those questions.

Suggested answers: This will depend on the issue chosen as the focus of the mind-map. Encourage learners to come up with at least three or four questions relating to the issue, and for each question, to think of at least one source that they could use to find answer.

Peer feedback (approx. 5–10 mins)

Pair learners with a partner from a different group. Learners give peer feedback on questions about their partner's mind-map.

Getting better at research skills: Lesson 9

In Lesson 9, learners focus on getting better at information skills, by considering the usefulness of different sources; conducting research, by deciding whether a prediction is correct on the basis of data collected in an investigation; and recording findings, by making decisions on how to present findings clearly.

CAMBRIDGE STAGE 6 RESEARCH LEARNING OBJECTIVES

1.2 Information skills: Identify sources and locate relevant information and answers to questions within them

1.3 Conducting research: Conduct investigations, using interviews or questionnaires to test a prediction or begin to answer a research question

1.4 Recording findings: Select, organise and record relevant information from sources and findings from research using an appropriate method

LESSON LEARNING GOALS

To get better at:

- giving reasons for choosing a source to help me find out about a topic

- deciding whether a prediction is correct as a result of carrying out an investigation

- choosing a way of clearly showing what I have learnt from my research.

Resources needed

Learner's Skills Book 6

Downloadable 1.13

Challenge topic (e.g. Keeping healthy, Moving goods and people)

Prior learning (approx. 5–10 mins)

Good for: Building on previous knowledge.

Activity: Ask learners to decide which would be the most useful source for finding out about a local issue by choosing from a list of options.

Ways of working: Learners can work individually at first, and then in pairs or small groups. Stage a plenary session, encouraging learners to share and respond to each other's ideas.

Differentiation: Support learners by asking them to focus on the last three options only and decide from those which would be the most useful. Check learners' understanding of the options by using questioning. Challenge learners to give reasons for choosing a particular option as the 'most useful'.

Suggested answers: The final option (Talk to parents . . .) is likely to be the most useful, as it is parents who make the final decision about how their children should go to school. Accept any reasonable suggestions for ordering the other options, especially where learners can give reasons to support their ideas.

Starter activity (approx. 10–15 mins)

Good for: Discussing the advantages of presenting findings in different formats and checking whether a prediction is correct based on the findings of an investigation.

Activity: Read through the learning goals for this lesson with learners at the beginning of this activity. Ask learners to read a short text about the background to an investigation before considering the advantages of presenting findings using a graph or a table. Learners then use the data to check the accuracy of a prediction.

Ways of working: Give learners the opportunity to work in pairs or small groups to discuss the questions before holding a class discussion. Encourage learners to share and respond to each other's ideas.

Differentiation: Support learners by checking their understanding of the text and the way findings have been presented alternatively in a graph and a table by using questioning. Challenge learners to give reasons for preferring either the bar chart or the table as a way of presenting the data.

Suggested answers: Accept any reasonable responses, especially where learners can offer reasons or evidence for their ideas. While some learners may prefer the bar chart because it shows the results 'at a glance' (i.e. in a clear visual form), others may prefer the table because it gives precise numbers for each response and allows other calculations to be made more easily (e.g. total number of families walking compared to families using their car). The prediction is correct, in that car use is more common among families living further away from the school. Allow time for some discussion of how Zara and Arun could use their findings to take action for change.

Main activity (approx. 15–20 mins)

Good for: Getting better at making decisions when planning an investigation.

Activity: Ask learners in small groups to decide on a local issue where they think change is needed, and to plan an investigation into it with a view to finding out what changes could be made.

Ways of working: Learners work in small groups, responding to the question prompts and recording their answers. Stage a plenary when this process has been completed, encouraging each group to report to the whole class, and allowing others the chance to respond.

Differentiation: Support learners by giving them an issue to focus on. Provide a short text for the learners to extract information from, using it to complete the question prompts in the Learner's Skills Book (see the Worked Example in Downloadable 1.13). Challenge learners to come up with their own issue, and to complete the question prompts with their own ideas about how to carry out an investigation into it.

Suggested answers: This will depend on the issue each group works on. Encourage groups to think practically about what sort of change might be achievable, rather than just what they would like to see. If time is available, give learners the opportunity to carry out the investigation they have planned.

Taking it further: Lessons 7–9

What local issues have your learners identified that they would like to change? Based on their work in Lesson 9, what further steps could be taken? Look for opportunities to arrange visits outside the classroom or to invite speakers into the classroom to enable learners to find out more about these local issues. Encourage learners to develop a response to their chosen issue by carrying out a course of action that they plan and deliver as a team project. Their response could include activities such as awareness-raising campaigns, fund-raising, action in the community, and so on. Give learners the opportunity to share the outcome of their project through class assemblies, parent evenings, poster or video presentations, and so on.

> Analysis

SKILLS SECTION	CROSS-CURRICULAR LINKS *Learners have opportunities to apply their knowledge and understanding of, and skills in:*	TOPICS MODELLED
Starting with	Science: thinking and working scientifically • Sort, group and classify objects, materials and living things through testing, observation and using secondary information • Use a range of secondary information sources to research and select relevant evidence to answer questions • Collect and record observations and/or measurements in tables and diagrams appropriate to the type of scientific enquiry • Describe patterns in results, including identifying any anomalous results Geography: human geography • Understanding how human activities cause environments to change • Understanding climate data • Selecting and interpreting information at different scales (local, national, global) Geography: physical geography • Understanding climate data Maths: statistics • Record, organise and represent categorical, discrete and continuous data • Choose and explain which representation to use in a given situation Language skills: reading • Distinguish between fact and opinion in a range of texts (speaking and listening) Language skills: speaking and listening • Structure information to aid the listener's understanding of the main and subsidiary points	Moving goods and people Keeping healthy Sharing Planet Earth
Developing	Geography: human geography • land use, economic activity, trade links) Maths: statistics • Record, organise and represent categorical, discrete and continuous data • Choose and explain which representation to use in a given situation	Moving goods and people Water, food and farming

SKILLS SECTION	CROSS-CURRICULAR LINKS *Learners have opportunities to apply their knowledge and understanding of, and skills in:*	TOPICS MODELLED
	Language skills: writing • Write balanced arguments, developing points logically and convincingly Science: thinking and working scientifically • Use a range of secondary information sources to research and select relevant evidence to answer questions • Collect and record observations and/or measurements in tables and diagrams appropriate to the type of scientific enquiry • Describe patterns in results, including identifying any anomalous results	
Getting better at	Geography: human geography • Land use, economic activity, trade links Language skills: writing • Develop writing for a purpose using language and features appropriate for a range of text types	Moving goods and people Water, food and farming

The cross-curricular links in this table are reproduced from Cambridge International curriculum frameworks. This Cambridge International copyright material is reproduced under licence and remains the intellectual property of Cambridge Assessment International Education.

Starting with analysis skills: Lesson 1

In Lesson 1, learners focus on starting to identify perspectives, by considering the differences between their own personal perspective, a local or national perspective, and global perspectives on a topic.

CAMBRIDGE STAGE 6 ANALYSIS LEARNING OBJECTIVES

2.1 Identifying perspectives: Identify some key points from different perspectives on the same topic within a source

LESSON LEARNING GOALS

To start to:
• recognise that there are differences in the ways different people think about a topic.

Resources needed

Learner's Skills Book 6

Downloadables 2.1 and 2.2

Challenge topic (e.g. Moving goods and people, Keeping healthy, Sharing Planet Earth)

Prior learning (approx. 5–10 mins)

Good for: Building on previous knowledge.

Activity: Ask learners to match the words to make pairs. Most pairs are made of words that are more or less opposite in meaning.

Ways of working: Give learners the opportunity to work individually on the task before putting them in pairs or small groups to discuss their work. Then stage a plenary session to check answers with the whole class.

Differentiation: Support learners by checking their understanding of the words by using questioning. Challenge learners to explain what connection they have found between each pair of words.

Suggested answers:

1   cause – consequence; global – local; fact – opinion; prediction – result; problem – solution

2   There are no definitive answers as learners will express a variety of personal perspectives on the topics under discussion.

Starter activity (approx. 10–15 mins)

Good for: Starting to explore personal perspectives on a topic and understanding that these may vary from person to person.

Activity: Read through the learning goals for this lesson with learners at the beginning of this activity. Ask learners to read the brief introduction to the activity and to identify the topic under discussion (eating meat / vegetarianism). They then choose another topic and make a note of their own personal perspective on it before asking others for their personal perspectives.

Ways of working: Learners work individually to identify their own personal perspective on a topic of their choice. They then mingle with other learners to exchange personal perspectives on different topics. Alternatively, learners can be re-grouped to carry out this part of the activity. A plenary session could be staged at the end of the activity, focusing on the variety of personal perspectives learners have found relating to their chosen topic.

Differentiation: Support learners by checking their understanding of the introduction to the activity by using questioning. Allow learners to continue to focus on the topic introduced in this part of the activity (eating meat / vegetarianism) when it comes to expressing their own personal perspective and eliciting personal perspectives from others. Challenge learners to choose a topic from the list provided and to explain their personal perspective (e.g. 'Why do they think the way they do about that topic?', 'Why might other people think differently?').

Suggested answers:

1   The topic is eating meat (Sofia) vs vegetarianism (Zara).

2   No definitive answer. Accept any reasonable response, especially if supported by evidence or reasoning.

3   Encourage learners to think about how local, national or even global factors might influence people's perspectives. If necessary, provide some alternative viewpoints on this topic to illustrate this (e.g. 'What would be the perspective of someone who lives in a country where the land and climate is more suited to raising animals than growing crops?', '. . . of someone who lives in a country where only the rich can afford to eat meat regularly, and many people do not get enough food?', etc.).

Main activity (approx. 20–25 mins)

Good for: Starting to understand the differences between personal, local/national and global perspectives on a topic.

Activity: Ask learners to re-visit the topic they chose in the Starter activity, this time identifying a local/national perspective and a global perspective relating to that topic.

Ways of working: Learners can work individually on completing the table before being put into pairs or small groups to discuss their work. (Alternatively, learners can be put into groups focusing on the same topic from the outset, so that they can reach a group consensus about a local/national and a global perspective on their chosen topic.) Stage a plenary session at the end of the activity, encouraging learners to share different perspectives on their chosen topics.

Differentiation: Support learners by checking their understanding of the differences between personal, local/national and global perspectives using the examples provided (A–C). (Further support can be offered by using the activity in Downloadable 2.2.) Challenge learners to think about who might say each of these statements about eating meat, and why. Further challenge learners by asking them to come up with local/national and global perspectives on their chosen topic when completing the table.

Suggested answers:

Part 1:

Perspective A: local/national (this perspective could be expressed by a government official in a country where meat production is an important part of the local economy; here, eating meat can be seen to have social benefits because of the income derived from it).

Perspective B: global (this perspective could be expressed by a scientist studying the causes of climate change, reflecting the impact that eating meat has on the environment generally).

Perspective C: personal (this perspective could be expressed by an individual, based on their own experience of eating meat).

Part 2: For possible answers for the topics of litter and public transport (as presented in the alternative matching activity in Downloadable 2.1), see Worked Example in Downloadable 2.2.

Peer feedback (approx. 5–10 mins)

Pair each learner with a partner from a different group. Ask them to look at each other's completed tables, and to give a YES/NO response to each of the questions, which should be recorded in their books. Where the response is 'No' to any of the questions, encourage partners to tell each other how the work could be improved. Time can be allowed for learners to carry out any necessary changes.

Starting with analysis skills: Lesson 2

In Lesson 2, learners focus on starting to make connections, by thinking about the types of problem that might affect them in their local environment; and on solving problems, by thinking of solutions to local problems.

Challenge topic (e.g. Moving goods and people, Keeping healthy, Sharing Planet Earth)

Prior learning (approx. 5–10 mins)

Good for: Building on previous knowledge.

Activity: Ask learners to identify personal, local/national and global perspectives from a list of perspectives on the same topic and to discuss these with a partner.

Ways of working: Learners can be given the opportunity to work individually on the task before being put into pairs or small groups to discuss their work. Stage a plenary session at the end of the activity to check answers with the whole class.

Differentiation: Support learners by checking their understanding of the perspectives in the list by using questioning. Challenge learners to explain their answers (e.g. 'Why do you think that this is a global perspective?') and to come up with more ideas about the causes and consequences of the problem, as well as possible solutions.

Suggested answers:

a   Personal

b   Global

c   Local/national

d   Global

e   Local/national

f   Personal

(See the Worked Example in Downloadable 2.3.)

CAMBRIDGE STAGE 6 ANALYSIS LEARNING OBJECTIVES

2.3   Making connections: Talk about simple causes of a local issue and consequences for others

2.4   Solving problems: Suggest and justify an action to make a positive difference to a local issue

LESSON LEARNING GOALS

To start to:

- talk about problems that affect people where I live and what causes them
- talk about how a local problem affects me and other people and what can be done about it.

Resources needed

Learner's Skills Book 6

Downloadables 2.3, 2.4, 2.5 and 2.6

1   Eating unhealthy food such as sugary snacks and sweets.

2   From the perspectives given here, three possible causes are advertising, availability in local shops and personal choice.

3   From the perspectives given here, possible consequences are health problems such as obesity, and pollution because of the type of packaging commonly used.

4   From the perspectives given here, a possible solution is to bring healthy snacks from home in re-usable containers.

Encourage learners to come up with other causes, consequences and solutions.

Starter activity (approx. 10–15 mins)

Good for: Starting to talk about how local problems affect people, and what their causes are.

Activity: Read through the learning goals for this lesson with learners at the beginning of this activity. Ask learners in groups to discuss causes, consequences and solutions relating to a local problem.

Ways of working: Put the learners into small groups and assign each group one of the problems mentioned by the characters in the introduction to this activity. Ask them to discuss the three questions about causes, consequences and solutions in their group. Follow this up with a class discussion in which groups report to the class on their responses to the questions and respond to other groups' ideas.

Differentiation: Support learners by checking their understanding of the problems by using questioning. Challenge learners to come up with more than one response to each of the three questions. In the class discussion, challenge learners to explain why they think their group's problem is the most important.

Suggested answers: There are no definitive answers to the questions. Accept a range of reasonable responses, especially those that are supported by reasoning or evidence. Some possible responses are given in the Worked Example in Downloadable 2.4.

Main activity (approx. 20–25 mins)

Good for: Starting to think about problems that affect people locally and what can be done to solve them.

Activity: Ask learners to use a mind-map to generate ideas about local problems that affect them personally (Downloadable 2.5 provides a template). Then ask them to identify the issue they think is the most important and to answer further questions about it.

Ways of working: Learners continue to work in small groups. At the end of the activity, stage a plenary session to give groups the opportunity to report to the whole class on their work and to hear how others respond to it.

Differentiation: Support learners by asking them to focus on one problem only, either of their own choice or one that you select for them. Challenge learners to come up with more than one local issue, and to justify their choice as to which one is the most important.

Suggested answers: There are no definitive answers. Accept any reasonable responses, especially those supported by reasoning and evidence. Some possible responses are given in the Worked Example in Downloadable 2.6; possible answers to the follow-on questions in this example might be:

1   Playing in the sun at break time when the weather's hot.

2   I like playing outdoors in the sun, but only for a limited time.

3   Children should have a choice when the weather's hot: play outside or stay indoors.

4   Teachers don't like being on playground duty in hot weather; parents want to protect children from the sun.

5   Some schools have shaded areas outdoors where children can sit in hot weather.

6   Create a shaded area for children and teachers to sit outside – this way, children get some fresh air, but don't become dehydrated or too tired.

Starting with analysis skills: Lesson 3

In Lesson 3, learners focus on starting to interpret data, by identifying patterns in – and drawing conclusions from – numerical data presented in charts and tables.

> CAMBRIDGE STAGE 6 ANALYSIS
> LEARNING OBJECTIVES
>
> 2.2 Interpreting data: Find and interpret simple patterns in graphical or numerical data

> LESSON LEARNING GOALS
>
> To start to:
> - find and describe patterns in data and say what they mean.

Resources needed

Learner's Skills Book 6

Downloadable 2.7

Challenge topic (e.g. Moving goods and people, Keeping healthy, Sharing Planet Earth)

Prior learning (approx. 5–10 mins)

Good for: Building on previous knowledge.

Activity: Ask learners to match problems with solutions and to think about their local impacts.

Ways of working: Learners can work individually on the task to begin with before getting into pairs or small groups to check their work and discuss their responses to the questions.

Differentiation: Support learners by checking their understanding of the problems and solutions in the list by using questioning. Challenge learners to explain their answers (e.g. 'How does this solution deal with the problem?') and to come up with further solutions to each problem.

Suggested answers: See Downloadable 2.7 for a Worked Example.

Starter activity (approx. 10–15 mins)

Good for: Starting to interpret numerical data presented in graphs by identifying patterns and explaining what they mean.

Activity: Read through the learning goals for this lesson with learners at the beginning of this activity. Ask learners to look at a bar chart and to talk about the patterns they can see in the data it presents and what these patterns mean.

Ways of working: Give learners the opportunity to talk about their ideas in pairs or small groups before staging a plenary session to discuss the answers to the questions.

Differentiation: Support learners by asking them to identify features of the bar chart (e.g. 'Point to the vertical axis.', 'What do these numbers mean?', 'Why are there two different colours?'). Challenge learners to identify and explain patterns in the data presented in the chart.

Suggested answers:

1   Check that learners understand that the maximum temperatures represent temperatures during the day; minimum temperatures represent temperatures at night.

    The chart shows an increase in average temperatures from February (the coldest month) to July (the hottest month), followed by a decrease from July to February. (There are five successive months of increase, followed by seven successive months of decrease.) The difference between the maximum and minimum daily temperatures is greater during the hottest months (June to September) than during the colder months. Temperatures tend to increase most rapidly from May to July: the biggest month-to-month increase is between June and July. The slowest rate of decrease is from November to February: the biggest month-to-month decrease is between September and October.

2   During the hottest months (June to September), it may be too hot to do many activities outdoors during the day; people may prefer to go out in the evening or at night when temperatures are cooler. For the rest of the year, the opposite may be true: daytime temperatures allow for being active during the day, but people may prefer to stay indoors in the evening or at night, especially during the coldest months (December to February).

Main activity (approx. 20–25 mins)

Good for: Starting to interpret numerical data presented in tables, and for comparing sets of data to understand their meaning.

Activity: Ask learners to look at two sets of data presented in tables and to make comparisons with the data presented in the Starter activity.

Ways of working: Learners can work in pairs or small groups to talk about the data in the tables. Give learners the opportunity to talk in pairs or small groups about the questions for a class discussion before staging a plenary session.

Differentiation: Support learners by checking their understanding of the data in the tables by using questioning (e.g. 'What differences can you see between the data for April and the data for May?', 'Are there the same differences between the data for May and the data for June?', etc.). Challenge learners to make connections between the patterns of data in the tables and the pattern of data in the bar chart.

Suggested answers:

1   Learners should look for patterns in the tables by reading across the rows. In the first table, this shows that, month by month, the number of journeys by car increases while the number of journeys on foot decreases. The reverse is true in the second table. (For other types of journey, there are small fluctuations in numbers, but no obvious pattern.)

    This could be explained by changes in temperature. The increase and decrease in the number of car journeys corresponds to the rise and fall in monthly average temperatures, as shown in the bar chart.

Possible answers to the class discussion questions:

1   The higher the monthly average temperature, the more parents consider it safer or less tiring for their children to travel to school by car; conversely, the cooler the temperatures, the more parents choose to let their children walk to school.

2   Accept any reasonable response, especially those supported by evidence or reasoning. For example, clearly some parents continue to drive their children to school throughout the year. They could be challenged to adopt the pattern of other parents, thereby increasing the number of children who walk to school during the cooler months, by pointing out the benefits of exercise for their children, while at the same time reducing traffic congestion and the impact on the environment in terms of air and noise pollution. Some schools have introduced 'walking buses' (groups of children walking to school under adult supervision) to improve safety. To increase the number of children who walk to school during the hotter months would be more challenging, but measures such as carrying water bottles and choosing more shaded routes could be suggested. Schools could provide supervision for children arriving on foot early to avoid hotter temperatures later in the day.

Taking it further: Lessons 1–3

What local issues have your learners identified? What are the local and/or national perspectives on those issues? Encourage learners to do further research to find out where else in the world the same issues exist. If possible, partner with schools in other countries – for example, using video conferencing to find out what issues are shared in common, how local and/or national perspectives on those issues vary from place to place, and what solutions have been found. Learners can then refine their ideas about solutions that could be applied to the local issues they have identified, and be given the opportunity to share what they have learnt through class assemblies, parent evenings, poster or video presentations, and so on.

Developing analysis skills: Lesson 4

In Lesson 4, learners focus on developing their skills at identifying perspectives, by looking at a range of perspectives on the same topic and by thinking of how the interests that different stakeholders have in a topic result in a variety of different perspectives.

CAMBRIDGE STAGE 6 ANALYSIS LEARNING OBJECTIVES

2.1 Identifying perspectives: Identify some key points from different perspectives on the same topic within a source

LESSON LEARNING GOALS

To develop my knowledge and understanding about:

- describing how different people – including myself – think and feel about a topic.

Resources needed

Learner's Skills Book 6

Downloadable 2.8, 2.9, 2.10 and 2.11

Challenge topic (e.g. Moving goods and people, Water, food and farming)

Prior learning (approx. 5–10 mins)

Good for: Building on previous knowledge.

Activity: Ask learners to sort four perspectives on the topic of air travel into personal and local/national perspectives, for or against the topic.

Ways of working: Learners work on the task individually to begin with before getting into pairs or small groups to discuss their work. Stage a plenary session to check the answers with the whole class.

Differentiation: Support learners by checking their understanding of each perspective by using questioning. Challenge learners to explain their answers (e.g. 'Why do you think this is a personal perspective on the topic?') and to come up with some global perspectives on the topic.

Suggested answers:

A   personal perspective/for

B   local/national perspective/against

C   personal perspective/against

D   local/national perspective/for

See Downloadable 2.8 for a Worked Example.

Global perspectives on air travel could include the impact on climate change (negative – aircraft produce a lot of carbon dioxide) and how it has helped to create a global community (positive – more people travel to and work in different countries around the globe; major tourist attractions and sporting events such as the Olympic Games can attract visitors from around the world).

Starter activity (approx. 10–15 mins)

Good for: Developing an understanding of how the perspectives of different people who have an interest in a topic can vary from one another and why.

Activity: Read through the learning goals for this lesson with learners at the beginning of this activity. Ask learners to read a short article on a topic and to identify the perspectives of different people who are affected by the topic either in negative or positive ways.

Ways of working: Learners can work independently on the task to begin with before getting into pairs or small groups to discuss their work. Give learners the opportunity to talk about the questions for the class discussion in their pairs or groups before staging a plenary session.

Differentiation: Support learners by checking their understanding of the perspectives by using questioning. If appropriate, reduce the number of perspectives learners have to match, including at least one negative and one positive perspective. Challenge learners to match all the perspectives and to come up with other possible perspectives, including their own personal perspective.

Suggested answers: See Downloadable 2.9 for a Worked Example for the diagram.

1   A consumer in Northland (likes being able to buy flowers at any time of the year); a farmer in the Southerly Islands (makes a profit from the trade).

2   An environmental campaigner (impact of the trade on climate change); a farm worker on the Southerly Islands (hard work, poor wages); a flower-grower in Northland (hard to compete against cheaper flowers from elsewhere).

(The position of the technology expert is less clear-cut – probably would be 'in favour of' if given the opportunity to develop a machine to harvest the flowers.)

3   Accept any reasonable suggestions; for example, a pilot working for the airline that flies the flowers to Northland (in favour of), a scientist concerned about the spread of plant disease or pests (against).

4   Encourage learners to share their personal perspectives with the class and to explain their reasons. Give learners the opportunity to respond to one another.

Main activity (approx. 20–25 mins)

Good for: Developing the idea of 'stakeholders' to focus learners' attention on how and why different people with an interest in a topic may have different perspectives on it.

Activity: Ask learners in pairs or groups to choose a different topic and to use a mind-map to identify stakeholders with an interest in that topic (Downloadable 2.10 provides a template). They then identify two contrasting stakeholder perspectives, as well as thinking about their own personal perspective and why they hold that view.

Ways of working: Learners continue working in pairs or small groups to identify stakeholders with an interest in a topic of their own choice. Stage a plenary session at the end of the activity to give learners the opportunity to report back to the whole class and respond to each other's ideas.

Differentiation: Support learners by helping them to identify a suitable topic (or by providing them with a topic that is of interest to them). Challenge learners to choose their own topic and to explain why they hold a particular personal perspective on that topic.

Suggested answers: There are no definitive answers: responses will depend on the learners' choices of topics.

Some possible responses for the public transport topic are given in the Worked Example in Downloadable 2.11; responses to the follow-on questions might be:

1   Car manufacturer – we won't sell as many cars if public transport is cheap and efficient. (negative)

2   City resident – public transport reduces the number of cars on our streets, so there's less noise and pollution. (positive)

3   I'd like to see more money spent on improving public transport in our city.

4   If public transport were better, I could use it to get to school every day.

Developing analysis skills: Lesson 5

In Lesson 5, learners focus on developing their skills at making connections, by thinking about the relationship between causes, consequences and solutions to local problems; and solving problems, by considering a range of practical actions that can be taken to solve a local issue and thinking about their own personal response to the issue.

CAMBRIDGE STAGE 6 ANALYSIS LEARNING OBJECTIVES	LESSON LEARNING GOALS
2.3 Making connections: Talk about simple causes of a local issue and consequences for others 2.4 Solving problems: Suggest and justify an action to make a positive difference to a local issue	To develop my knowledge and understanding about: • explaining the causes of local problems and how they affect people • discussing the actions I could take to help solve a local problem.

Resources needed

Learner's Skills Book 6

Downloadable 2.12

Challenge topic (e.g. Moving goods and people, Water, food and farming)

Prior learning (approx. 5–10 mins)

Good for: Building on previous knowledge.

Activity: Ask learners to match causes, consequences and solutions to three issues related to pollution.

Ways of working: Learners can work on the task individually to begin with before getting into pairs or small groups to discuss their work. Stage a plenary session to check answers with the whole class.

Differentiation: Support learners by checking their understanding of the descriptions of causes, consequences and solutions by using questioning. Where appropriate, ask learners to pick just one of the issues and to identify its cause, consequence and solution. Challenge learners to explain their answers, and to come up with additional consequence and solutions for each of the issues.

Suggested answers: See the Worked Example in Downloadable 2.12.

Other consequences could include:

*   noise pollution – damage to hearing among workers at the airport (solution: workers wear ear protection)
*   plastic pollution – harm to wildlife (solution: pick up litter and remove from environment)
*   air pollution – sports events cancelled (solution: ban traffic from city centres).

This is not an exhaustive list. Encourage learners to come up with further consequences and solutions, especially those that are appropriate in their own local environment.

Starter activity (approx. 10–15 mins)

Good for: Developing ideas about what action to take in response to a local problem.

Activity: Read through the learning goals for this lesson with learners at the beginning of this activity. Ask learners to read a list of actions that could be taken in response to a local problem, and to discuss their pros and cons.

Ways of working: Give learners the opportunity to discuss each of the proposed actions in pairs or small

groups and to decide on which action they think would be the most effective. In each pair or group, one learner could record the pros and cons of each action. Stage a plenary session in which pairs or groups share their ideas with the whole class and respond to each other's ideas.

Differentiation: Support learners by checking their understanding of the proposed actions by using questioning. Where appropriate, limit the number of actions that learners discuss from the list. Challenge learners to come up with a number of different pros and cons for each action and to reach a group consensus on which action they think would be the most effective. Encourage learners to give reasons in support of their decision.

Suggested answers:

1 and 2 The following is a list of suggestions, not definitive answers. Accept any reasonable responses from learners, especially those supported by evidence or reasoning.

Action	Pros	Cons
1 Make a 'No Stopping' zone	Reduces the amount of traffic and emissions from cars	Difficult to enforce
2 Put up posters	Children could make their own posters	Drivers might be distracted by posters, risking accidents
3 Plant a 'green wall'	Provides a natural solution	Would cost money to install, and take time to grow
4 Provide all children with anti-smog masks	Gives children protection from breathing in pollution	Would cost money
5 Give a presentation to the whole school	Informs people about the problem	May not result in any action being taken
6 Reward children who walk to school or use public transport	Encourages people to use cars less	Doesn't change adults' behaviour

3   Accept any reasonable responses, especially those supported by evidence or reasoning. Encourage learners to discuss solutions that would be appropriate in their own local setting.

4   Accept any reasonable responses, especially those supported by evidence or reasoning. One approach to dealing with this question could be to ask each group to 'champion' one of the proposed actions (i.e. to put forward arguments in support of it) and stage a class debate, culminating in a vote.

Main activity (approx. 20–25 mins)

Good for: Developing ideas about how to justify choosing a course of action and considering personal responses to a local issue.

Activity: Ask learners to read the brief introduction to the activity and the paragraph written as a justification for a chosen course of action. They then analyse the arguments used in the justification, before making some personal decisions about actions to be taken.

Ways of working: Give learners the opportunity to discuss their ideas about the justification in pairs or small groups before staging the class discussion. Learners can then work individually on their responses to the two follow-up questions before getting into pairs to give each other peer feedback on their work.

Differentiation: Support learners by checking their understanding of the justification paragraph by using questioning. Challenge learners to come up with their

own personal decisions about further actions to be taken.

Suggested answers:

Possible answers to the class discussion questions:

1   a   Risk to young people's health from air pollution.

    b   Learners exposed to risk when travelling to and from school.

2   a   Protects users from 90 percent of air pollution.

    b   Might help to change drivers' behaviour.

    c   Shows that the school cares.

Possible responses for the questions in Part 2:

1   I would suggest that the school could raise funds to pay for the masks by holding a Quiz Night, inviting teams of learners and parents to take part.

2   I could suggest to my parents that we use the car less and walk more often, or take public transport whenever possible.

Peer feedback (approx. 5–10 mins)

Pair each learner with a partner from a different group. Ask them to look at each other's completed responses and to give a YES/NO response to each of the questions, which should be recorded in their books. Where the response is 'No' to any of the questions, encourage partners to tell each other how the work could be improved. Time can be allowed for learners to carry out any necessary changes.

Developing analysis skills: Lesson 6

In Lesson 6, learners focus on developing their skills at interpreting data, by describing and comparing patterns in two sets of numerical data.

CAMBRIDGE STAGE 6 ANALYSIS LEARNING OBJECTIVES

2.2 Interpreting data: Find and interpret simple patterns in graphical or numerical data

LESSON LEARNING GOALS

To develop my knowledge and understanding about:

- finding patterns in data and explaining what they mean.

Resources needed

Learner's Skills Book 6

Challenge topic (e.g. Moving goods and people, Water, food and farming)

Prior learning (approx. 5–10 mins)

Good for: Building on previous knowledge.

Activity: Ask learners to look at some numerical data presented in a bar chart and to draw some conclusions from it.

Ways of working: Learners can work individually on the task at first before getting into pairs or small groups to discuss their work. Stage a plenary session to check answers with the whole class.

Differentiation: Support learners by helping them to identify features of the bar chart (e.g. 'Point to the vertical axis. What do these numbers show?', 'Why are there bars of different colours?', etc.). Encourage learners to identify which conclusions are correct and to explain how they know this. Challenge learners to draw further conclusions from the data and to predict what the results for the 10–18 age group would show.

Suggested answers:

1   a   CORRECT (for both men and women, the bars show that the greater the age, the less time spent online)

     b   INCORRECT (in the oldest age group, men spend more time online than women)

     c   INCORRECT (the bars for these two groups (Men 18–34 and Women 35–54) are of equal height, suggesting that they spend the same amount of time online

     d   CORRECT (Women 55+ spend just over 2 hours online daily; Women 18–34 spend over 4 hours)

2   Other conclusions could include the fact that the time spent online by women decreases more rapidly as they get older than it does for men; the difference in the amount of time spent online by men and women is greatest in the youngest age group, but narrows after that, and so on.

3   Accept any reasonable responses, especially those supported by evidence or reasoning. Predictions can be checked by carrying out a survey.

Starter activity (approx. 10–15 mins)

Good for: Developing an understanding of how to report patterns in data collected in a survey, and of how to improve questionnaire design in order to collect data more efficiently.

Activity: Read through the learning goals for this lesson with learners at the beginning of this activity.

Ask learners to use a questionnaire to carry out a quick survey among other learners. They then report on their findings and comment on the design of the questionnaire.

Ways of working: Learners work in pairs or small groups to carry out a survey using a questionnaire. This can be done by letting learners mingle, or by re-grouping them. Give learners the opportunity to discuss the questions for the class discussion in their pairs or groups. Then stage a plenary in which learners can report back to the whole class and respond to each other's ideas.

Differentiation: Support learners by checking their understanding of the questionnaire and how to use it to carry out a survey by using questioning (e.g. 'What question will you ask first?', ' How will you record the response?', 'Will you ask everyone the second question?', etc.). Challenge learners to make predictions about the likely outcome of the survey and to report the patterns they find in their actual results.

Suggested answers:

1   Accept any reasonable responses, especially those supported by evidence or reasoning.

2   Encourage learners to look for patterns rather than just report their results (e.g. 'Television is the most popular way of getting the news' or 'The number of children getting the news online was half that of children watching the news on television').

Possible answers to the class discussion questions:

1   As above, encourage learners to report patterns in their data. In a quick survey like this, results may be skewed by the small size of the sample. Encourage learners to say how the results of the survey could be made more reliable (e.g. by increasing the size of the sample).

2   Encourage learners to give reasons for the accuracy of their prediction (e.g. 'Newspapers and radio are not popular among children of my age', 'Families often watch the news together on TV', 'Not all children have their own computer, but every home has a TV', etc.)

3   If learners struggle to come up with their own ideas, draw their attention to fact that all the 'traditional' news media (television, radio, newspapers) can now be accessed online, so it may be confusing to use 'online' as a heading or category on its own. People also go online to get news via social media, from 'official' news outlets or from friends and family.

4   Encourage learners to discuss the importance of being aware of what is going on in the wider world, especially in an age of global communications when all parts of the world are interconnected. Elicit examples of how things that have happened in the news recently are affecting the lives of people in your local area.

Main activity (approx. 20–25 mins)

Good for: Developing an understanding of how to find and compare patterns in different sets of data.

Activity: Ask learners to look at two bar charts presenting numerical data for two different sets of respondents. They compare ways in which the patterns in the data are similar and different, and consider how the data could be used to support a course of action.

Ways of working: Learners in pairs or small groups discuss and compare the two charts. Give learners the opportunity to discuss the questions for the class discussion in their pairs or groups. At the end of the activity, stage a plenary session for learners to report back to the whole class and discuss their responses to the questions.

Differentiation: Support learners by helping them to identify features of the bar charts (e.g. 'Point to the horizontal axis. What do these numbers mean?', etc.). Challenge learners to find similarities and differences between the two sets of data and to explain them.

Suggested answers:

1   For both adults and children:

- television is the most popular way of following the news
- radio is the second least popular way of following the news.

Differences between the two sets of data:

- traditional news media (television, radio, newspapers) are used by higher percentages of adults than children
- children rely more on family and friends to get the news than adults do
- when getting the news online, adults use social media more than other online sources – the reverse is true for children
- newspapers are the least popular way of getting the news among children – the percentage of adults using newspapers is more than double that of children.

This is not an exhaustive list. Accept any other reasonable responses.

2   The bar charts show that Zara divided the 'online' category into two different ways of getting the news online (via social media, or by other means). She also added the category 'Family and friends' to include news being passed on by 'word of mouth' (although family and friends contacting each other via social media could also be included here).

3   The data could be used to show that quite a lot of children already follow the news in various ways, so it isn't just something that only adults do. The data also shows the greater importance of 'non-traditional' news media (such as going online) for children, which might make following the news more attractive to others.

Taking it further: Lessons 4–6

From Lesson 4, encourage learners to script and perform short dramatic dialogues between pairs of stakeholders whose interests are either aligned or opposed in the flower trade. Where interests are opposed, what solutions can be found?

Encourage learners to develop the idea of trade relationships between different countries – for example, by using research to create and annotate a map of the trade links between your country and other countries, showing what goods are imported or exported. Alternatively, annotate a world map to show which countries are the main exporters of a particular product or resource – for example, oil – and which countries are the main importers.

From Lesson 6, encourage learners to carry out a more wide-reaching investigation outside the classroom into which media people use for following the news. This could involve conducting a survey among their family members and relatives, for example. Research questions could focus on how much time people spend each day following the news, or on which media people think are the most reliable as news sources. Encourage learners to record and present their findings – for example, as a poster or slide show – to promote messages encouraging their peers to spend more time following the news, or to use more reliable news sources, and so on.

Getting better at analysis skills: Lesson 7

In Lesson 7, learners focus on getting better at identifying different perspectives, by classifying given perspectives on an issue as being in favour for or being against (or neutral). They consider how strongly these views are expressed and identify language that conveys this strength of support/opposition.

CAMBRIDGE STAGE 6 ANALYSIS LEARNING OBJECTIVES

2.1 Identifying perspectives: Identify some key points from different perspectives on the same topic within a source

LESSON LEARNING GOALS

To get better at:

- identifying some different ways that people can think about an issue
- recognising words that show the strength of feeling about an issue.

Resources needed

Learner's Skills Book 6

Downloadables 2.13 and 2.14

Challenge topic (e.g. Moving goods and people, Water, food and farming)

Prior learning (approx. 5 mins)

Good for: Keeping active the notion that skills development in Global Perspectives is in the final analysis centred on taking appropriate action.

Activity: Learners consider to what extent they are clear on what issue they will be addressing, what action they will take and what different perspectives they have (or will have to) consider.

Ways of working: This activity is probably best addressed individually prior to the class discussion. Encourage learners to be honest; they will be familiar with Marcus, Zara, Arun and Sofia's attempts to define issues, goals and perspectives to varying degrees of success.

Differentiation: Support learners by displaying images/text relevant to local issues. Challenge learners to deepen their justification for the issue chosen, goal set and the action proposed and to clearly link their ideas to different local perspectives.

Suggested answers: Refer the class to Arun's issue in Lesson 5. To what extent did Arun justify taking action on this issue? To what extent did his arguments justify the solution of wearing anti-smog masks? To what extent did he take into account different perspectives? They could point to one end of the class or another on a continuum (very well/not at all). How could he have improved?

Starter activity (approx. 10 mins)

Good for: Developing understanding that views on an issue (in this case the flower trade) aren't limited to 'for' or 'against'.

Activity: Read through the learning goals for this lesson with learners at the beginning of this activity. Ask learners to classify the following perspectives as: Strongly against, Somewhat against, Neutral, Somewhat in favour, Strongly in favour.

1   The working conditions are an absolute scandal; these heartless farmers are just making money out of other people's misery.

2   It is essential for my florist shop that flowers are available at any time of year. People need them for their special occasions.

3   Moving people and goods by air has a downside. Carbon is released.

4   Flowers grown in cooler climates cost more to produce because they have to be grown indoors.

5   Transporting flowers by air is an essential part of a key industry that is the cornerstone of our islands' prosperity.

6   It is possible for flowers to be harvested by machines.

Ways of working: Read out the first perspective or distribute Downloadable 2.13. Establish that the first perspective is strongly against.

Differentiation: Support learners by pointing out vocabulary choices that clarify for/against/neutral (e.g. 'has a downside' suggests 'against'). If learners still find this challenging, they could annotate the views with ☺ 'for', ☺ 'neutral', ☹ 'against' prior to deciding the strength of the opinion. Challenge learners to justify their decisions with reference to the vocabulary used, for example 'absolute scandal' 'heartless' 'misery' suggests strong opposition. How could they apply vocabulary choices like this to persuade people to take action on their issue? (NB the use of language is also considered in Evaluation Lesson 3)

Suggested answers: See the Worked Example in Downloadable 2.14.

Possible answers to the class discussion questions:

1   Arguments that are strongly against the trade emphasise the negative impacts – to the exclusion of any possible benefits.

2   Words or phrases used to emphasise the strength of negative feeling include: 'absolute scandal'; heartless'; 'making money out of other people's misery'.

3   Arguments that are strongly for the trade emphasise the benefits – to the exclusion of any possible drawbacks.

4   Words or phrases used to emphasise the strength of positive feeling include: 'essential', 'cornerstone of our [island's] prosperity'.

5   The words or phrases learners could use to emphasise the strength of their feelings about their issue will, of course, vary depending on their issue and your learners' individual perspectives. Look for consistency. You could ask learners to rank themselves on a scale of 1 to 10 – where 1 is strongly against and 10 is strongly in favour. This will assist you in assessing the extent to which the language they have selected to express their opinion is appropriate.

Main activity (approx. 20–25 mins)

Good for: Learners to apply their understanding of different perspectives (Strongly against, Somewhat against, Neutral, Somewhat in favour, Strongly in favour) in a different context.

Activity: In Lesson 4, learners were introduced to a range of perspectives on the same topic, and they learnt that the interests that different stakeholders have in a

topic results in a variety of different perspectives. They now re-visit these perspectives and suggest how they could be expressed to show appropriate depth of feeling on the issue.

Ways of working: Learners could be allocated particular perspectives to role play.

Differentiation: Support learners by modelling how different people might express support/opposition to a proposal appropriately on an issue with which they are familiar. Challenge learners to develop their justification by using a range of appropriate vocabulary/facts/perspectives to support their case.

Suggested answers: Responses from a haulage contractor might be as follows:

1   Congestion charging.

2   As a haulage contractor, he was opposed to the scheme.

3   It will cost £100 a day. Journey times will be increased. The measure will come into effect this year. Jobs could be lost if transport companies go out of business.

4   The £100 a day *is an absolute scandal*. Transporting goods by lorry *is an essential part of a key industry that is the cornerstone of our* city's *prosperity*. *It is essential* for the automotive industry *that* components *are available* reliably. The production lines *need* them to keep running.

5–7 Check that the answers to questions 5–7 express an opposing perspective.

Peer feedback (approx. 10 mins)

Pair each learner with a partner from a different group. Ask them to think about their ability to express a clear perspective, whether they provided appropriate information to support their case, whether they used appropriate language to successfully convince.

Getting better at analysis skills: Lesson 8

In Lesson 8, learners focus on making connections, by considering the consequences of a solution to a range of people who may have different perspectives; and on solving problems, by considering the impact of solutions on different people. They find out about solving problems through suggesting and justifying an action to make a positive difference to a local issue.

CAMBRIDGE STAGE 6 ANALYSIS LEARNING OBJECTIVES

2.3 Making connections: Talk about simple causes of a local issue and consequences for others

2.4 Solving problems: Suggest and justify an action to make a positive difference to a local issue

LESSON LEARNING GOALS

To get better at:

- developing ideas about how I would solve a local problem
- considering pros and cons for different people about ways to solve a local problem.

Resources needed

Learner's Skills Book 6

Downloadable 2.15

Challenge topic (e.g. Moving goods and people, Water, food and farming)

Highlighters and coloured pens

Prior learning (approx. 5–10 mins)

Good for: Scaffolding learners' understanding of how a solution arises. When advocating a particular solution, we may be influenced by many considerations, for example ethical or practical. In order to secure support for a particular solution, we may have to convince others who do not share our perspective that it is the most appropriate.

Activity: Learners investigate Marcus's solution to the transport issue by evaluating the perspectives that underpin it.

Ways of working: Give learners time to note their answer before taking suggestions.

Differentiation: Support learners by showing them how to use different coloured pencils/highlighters for each question and highlight the text appropriately. Challenge learners to role play how Marcus could respond to a deep sceptic to his idea.

Suggested answers:

1   Congestion/sustainable transport.

2   Cycling is a solution.

3   Safe storage would help.

4   He is a keen cyclist.

5   Local street is noisy. Cars cause congestion and pollution whereas bikes don't.

6   Cycling is sustainable, healthy, reduces congestion and is quieter.

Starter activity (approx. 10–15 mins)

Good for: Learners to use the processes modelled in the Prior learning activity in order to further develop their own perspective/solution.

Activity: Read through the learning goals for this lesson with learners at the beginning of this activity. Learners write about their proposed solution to their issue using Marcus's solution as a scaffold.

Ways of working: The activity requires some individual reflection time before answering the questions.

Differentiation: Support learners by identifying features of Marcus's model. Challenge learners to refine their writing by suggesting that they are trying to convince the kind of sceptic/naysayer we encountered in the previous activity.

Suggested answers:

1   My issue is energy.

2   I feel passionate about this because I know the damage caused by fossil fuels, which have been linked to climate change and pollution.

3   I want our school to invest in solar panels.

4   I know our school has a large roof and I think we could make a difference.

5   I searched on 'solar for schools' and found out that over 25 years, we could save nearly 750 tonnes of CO_2!

6 We have a big flat roof. We know that solar panels work. Not only does it save 750 tonnes of CO_2, it could also save the school £100,000 or $125,000 or RS95,000,000!

Main activity (approx. 20–25 mins)

Good for: Considering the consequences of a solution on others.

Activity: Learners are given a Worked Example (Downloadable 2.15) of how to consider different perspectives. They use this as a model to consider potential support for/opposition to their own proposal.

Ways of working: Learners work in groups, with individuals within the group tasked with considering the impact on a specific group (e.g. younger children) and reporting back. Specified areas for individuals to work on could be highlighted on the download to ensure a balance.

Differentiation: Support learners by highlighting words/ phrases from the modelled example that would be equally appropriate to their response. Challenge learners to consider that groups of people, for example 'parents', are in themselves diverse. Implications of any given solution may therefore vary accordingly.

Suggested answers: See the Worked Example in Downloadable 2.15. Possible responses to the follow-up questions in the class discussion based on the example in Downloadable 2.15 are:

1 Gardening can be fun, but it is important to make sure enough fruit and vegetables are available and variety is needed. It is also hard work and takes time.

2 It depends very much on the land made available and how well it is used. It needs time, hard work and knowledge.

3 Staff in the canteen may need to use new recipes. Children may need to try new food they're not used to. Parents and other adults in the community could come and help in ways they are not used to. Many people may need to learn new skills.

4 School gardening is sustainable. It gives children valuable new skills for the future. It is a good way of bringing young and old together.

Getting better at analysis skills: Lesson 9

In Lesson 9, learners focus on getting better at interpreting data, by considering not only what can be known for sure from a set of data, but also what can be inferred. They consider how survey results can clarify how perspectives differ on solutions to an issue, and use findings as part of a justification of an action to make a positive difference, making connections between local and global problems.

LESSON LEARNING GOALS

To get better at:

- describing in some detail the differences in the ways people think about a topic

- saying how other people's ways of thinking about a topic differ from my own, and why

- using a pattern found in data to support an argument and explaining why

- finding connections between local and global problems.

CAMBRIDGE STAGE 6 ANALYSIS LEARNING OBJECTIVES

2.1 Identifying perspectives: Identify some key points from different perspectives on the same topic within a source

2.2 Interpreting data: Find and interpret simple patterns in graphical or numerical data

2.3 Making connections: Talk about simple causes of a local issue and consequences for others

2.4 Solving problems: Suggest and justify an action to make a positive difference to a local issue

Resources needed

Learner's Skills Book 6

Downloadables 2.16, 2.17 and 2.18

Challenge topic (e.g. Moving goods and people, Water, food and farming)

If possible – survey data that the class have collected (see Downloadable 2.16 for ideas)

Prior learning (approx. 5 mins)

Good for: Formative assessment on learners' data-handling skills.

Activity: Learners look again at a set of data that they have used earlier in the unit and classify a series of statements by the following criteria:

- true statements (T)
- possibly true statements (PT)
- false statements (F).

Ways of working: This could be conducted individually or in pairs. It is best set up as a quick 'beat the clock' challenge. Remind children of your school's e-safety policy – especially with regard to the use of social media.

Differentiation: Support learners by pointing out that, while we know percentages, we don't know the numbers of adults and children surveyed. Challenge learners to create statements of their own for each category.

Suggested answers:

True statements: A, D

Possibly true statements: C, E

False statements: B

Starter activity (approx. 10 mins)

Good for: Learners to consider what can be learnt from a set of data about different perspectives on a range of solutions.

Activity: Read through the learning goals for this lesson with learners at the beginning of this activity. Following a Worked Example in the Learner's Skills Book, learners consider what can be learnt with certainty from a set of data, and what can reasonably be inferred.

Ways of working: Learners work individually in the first instance, with preparation for the class discussion being conducted initially in pairs. Supportive pairs could be used with those whose data-handling strategies are more secure supporting those whose understanding of appropriate strategies is less developed by explaining their methods.

Differentiation: Support learners by working closely with those whose understanding is less secure – especially if they do not initially understand appropriate calculation strategies. Challenge learners to justify their answers. What have they experienced that leads them to their conclusion?

Suggested answers: For a Worked Example of the table, see Downloadable 2.16.

Main activity (approx. 20–25 mins)

Good for: Learners to evaluate how well an action has been justified.

Activity: Learners consider the respective merits of four different justifications (provided in Downloadable 2.17). They then apply this understanding to creating a justification of their own.

Ways of working: The initial evaluation would lend itself to paired discussion. The justification will provide summative assessment of the learners' understanding of this unit and is therefore best done individually.

Differentiation: Support learners by encouraging them to use each of the factors in the table as success criteria for their own writing. Challenge learners to deepen their explanation for potential strengths/weaknesses of the action, for example by considering the impact on diverse people.

Suggested answers: See the Worked Example in Downloadable 2.18. For the justification part of the activity, the topic of water might produce the following responses:

The topic I am working on today is water.

My proposed action is installing water butts at school to collect rainwater.

This action would be a positive change because collecting rainwater saves a precious resource.

I know that different people would benefit from this action because parents would like to see their children developing good habits. Staff at the school could use this as a resource to teach about conservation, and maybe to grow food. Children could enjoy using the water collected to water plants.

The benefits of this approach are that firstly, rainwater contains nitrates and organic material that plants like.

In addition, rainwater does not contain salts, minerals and chemicals common in tap water.

There are, however, limitations to this approach because there can be problems with bacteria if the roof is not clean, and mosquitos breed if the water is not carefully covered.

However, overall, it can be seen that if it is carefully managed, water butts can help the school to be more sustainable.

Taking it further: Lessons 7–9

The issue of the flower trade (Lesson 7) could be used as a stimulus for learners to independently investigate geographical questions, issues and concepts surrounding the production of goods for export. Learners could be given opportunities to describe/present and explain their findings, make judgements and draw conclusions about how ethical/sustainable a particular trade is. Learners could be given opportunities to evaluate their own and others' findings.

> Evaluation

SKILLS SECTION	CROSS-CURRICULAR LINKS *Learners have opportunities to apply their knowledge and understanding of, and skills in:*	TOPICS MODELLED
Starting with	Science: thinking and working scientifically • Sort, group and classify objects, materials and living things through testing, observation and using secondary information • Use a range of secondary information sources to research and select relevant evidence to answer questions Language skills: writing • Develop writing of a range of text types for a specified audience, using appropriate content and language • Use organisational features appropriate to the text type, e.g. bulleted and numbered lists	Keeping healthy
Developing	Science: thinking and working scientifically • Sort, group and classify objects, materials and living things through testing, observation and using secondary information • Use a range of secondary information sources to research and select relevant evidence to answer questions Language skills: reading • Explore explicit meanings in a range of texts • Explore implicit meanings in a range of texts • Comment on how different viewpoints are expressed in texts	Keeping healthy
Getting better at	Science: thinking and working scientifically • Sort, group and classify objects, materials and living things through testing, observation and using secondary information • Use a range of secondary information sources to research and select relevant evidence to answer questions Language skills: reading • Explore explicit meanings in a range of texts • Explore implicit meanings in a range of texts • Identify, discuss and compare the purposes and features of different non-fiction text types, including balanced written arguments • Comment on how readers might react differently to the same text, depending on where or when they are reading it Geography: • Selecting and evaluating sources to decide on their relevance for investigations at a local scale	Reduce, re-use, recycle

The cross-curricular links in this table are reproduced from Cambridge International curriculum frameworks. This Cambridge International copyright material is reproduced under licence and remains the intellectual property of Cambridge Assessment International Education.

Starting with evaluation skills: Lesson 1

In Lesson 1, learners focus on starting to evaluate sources by identifying different sources of information and thinking about their potential uses. They begin to differentiate between those that provide facts and those that give access to different perspectives (by providing opinions).

CAMBRIDGE STAGE 6 EVALUATION LEARNING OBJECTIVES

3.1 Evaluating sources: Discuss a source, considering the author and/or purpose, and comment on its strengths and limitations

---

LESSON LEARNING GOALS

To start to:

- say what the purpose of a source is
- describe some of the features of the source
- recognise why a source may be useful.

Resources needed

Learner's Skills Book 6

Downloadables 3.1 and 3.2

Challenge topic (e.g. Keeping healthy)

Sources of information used elsewhere in the curriculum

Sources of information relevant to the issue your learners will be taking action on – alternatively you could follow the issue of healthy eating modelled by the characters in the Learner's Skills Book and provide similar resources to the ones they suggest

Prior learning (approx. 10 mins)

Good for: Helping learners to quickly activate their prior understanding of the range of sources of information they are familiar with and how different sources of information have been useful in different ways.

Activity: Learners generate lists of sources of information that they have used.

Ways of working: Learners initially write their own list. A tight time limit (e.g. 'how many can you think of in

one minute?') would provide a brisk start to the lesson. You could even divide this further (e.g. 'you have ten seconds to write down any source of information you have used in science'). Learners could have books that they have used in other subjects to hand. Give them a tight time limit to compare lists with a partner.

Differentiation: Support learners by having sources that have already been used on prominent display. Challenge learners to include as wide a range of subjects as possible in the time. For the class discussion, support learners by sticking to facts that can be found out (e.g. 'Which source would we use to tell us the temperature in (named place)?', 'Which source would we use to find the meaning of the word evaporation?'). Challenge learners to suggest sources that would give us different people's perspectives, for example 'Name me a source that we could use to find different perspectives about (named event in History).'

Suggested answers:

Source	Subject	Could it give us facts?	Could it give us perspectives?
The Natural World book	Science	Yes (e.g. about the water cycle).	Sometimes (e.g. people used to ridicule Copernicus' ideas).
[My Country] in the 19th Century	History	Yes (e.g. dates of key events).	Yes (e.g. different views on the causes of events).
Junior Atlas	Geography	Yes (e.g. rainfall statistics).	Not really.
Improve your skills video	PE	Yes (e.g. rules of the game).	Possible (e.g. different ideas about good technique).

Starter activity (approx. 5 mins)

Good for: Activating learners' understanding of different text purposes.

Activity: Read through the learning goals for this lesson with learners at the beginning of this activity. Learners match some texts to their purpose.

Ways of working: This could be completed individually or in pairs.

Differentiation: Support learners by narrowing down the choices. They could put an 'F' next to the purely factual first. Alternatively, challenge learners to provide other sources to meet the same purpose.

Suggested answers: See Downloadable 3.1 for a Worked Example. For the challenge activity, other possible sources might be as follows:

Purpose	Other possible source (challenge)
to outline the characteristics of something, (e.g. 'dinosaurs', 'ancient Benin')	specialist magazine
to change people's minds about something	opinion piece in a newspaper
to tell someone how to make something	recipe
to explain how or why something happens	a page in a science text book, (e.g. about the digestive system)
to give arguments and information from different points of view	meeting notes before a decision has been taken

Main activity (approx. 25–30 mins)

Good for: Helping learners to understand the use of different kinds of information when planning an action.

Activity: Learners suggest how Zara could use suggested sources to meet her goal of encouraging healthy eating in her class. They then discuss the usefulness of the various sources.

Ways of working: This could be completed individually or in pairs. Then lead into a class discussion; the question 'What source has been most useful to you in

suggesting appropriate action to take on your issue?' could be targeted to individuals or 'cold called' (i.e. by random name selection).

Differentiation: Support learners by suggesting that they begin their answers 'to give facts about . . . to give opinions about . . . so that . . . '. Challenge learners to discuss the advantages/disadvantages of the various sources (see the suggested answers table below). In the class discussion, support learners by asking them to identify relevant facts they have found on their issue. Challenge learners to develop their answers by suggestion appropriate action they have ascertained from their sources that might help resolve the issue they have identified.

Suggested answers: See Downloadable 3.2 for a Worked Example of the fill-in tables for Zara's and the learners' own sources. For the optional differentiation activity, advantages/disadvantages might include:

Source	Advantages/disadvantages (challenge)
Recipe for an avocado smoothie	☺ This is practical information and would have an end product. ☹ What if children still didn't like them?
Encyclopedia entry on 'healthy diet'	☺ There's no point making something that isn't healthy & this can give solid facts. ☹ Not everything will be listed and facts on their own don't persuade.
Leaflet from a vegan group	☺ Persuasive phrases could be 'magpied'. ☹ Not all healthy food is vegan. Not all vegan food is healthy.
Website on the pros and cons of being vegetarian	☺ It would be a good model text. ☹ Not all healthy food is vegetarian and some children might be put off. Not all vegetarian food is healthy.

Starting with evaluation skills: Lesson 2

In Lesson 2, learners focus on starting to apply evaluation skills by analysing the features of sources of information and considering their usefulness in respect of their topic goals.

> ### CAMBRIDGE STAGE 6 EVALUATION LEARNING OBJECTIVES
>
> 3.1 Evaluating sources: Discuss a source, considering the author and/or purpose and comment on its strengths and limitations

> ### LESSON LEARNING GOALS
>
> To start to:
>
> * recognise some strong points about a source
>
> * recognise some limitations of a source.

Resources needed

Learner's Skills Book 6

Challenge topic (e.g. Keeping healthy)

Sources gathered relevant to the challenge topic. Collecting these could be set as a homework activity. If the school has access to a library, a visit to it prior to the lesson could be used for gathering. Similarly, ICT resources could be searched in advance. Alternatively, information gathering could be set as a preparatory homework activity

Relevant images for the challenge topic(s)

Prior learning (approx. 5 mins)

Good for: Building on previous knowledge.

Activity: Ask learners to evaluate the usefulness of an advertisement for an obviously high sugar fizzy drink to Zara's goal.

Ways of working: Give learners time to consider their own view prior to opening this up to class discussion.

Differentiation: Support learners by asking them closed questions before probing (e.g. 'is this a healthy drink?', 'What is Zara's goal?') Challenge learners to explain

how Zara could use techniques in the advert (e.g. use of strong colour) to support a very different message.

Suggested answers: Zara wouldn't use the advert as it gives the wrong message. She could make an advert for an avocado smoothie in a similar attractive style.

Starter activity (approx. 10–15 mins)

Good for: Orientating the learners to their own challenge topic.

Activity: Read through the learning goals for this lesson with learners at the beginning of this activity. Learners identify their topic area. They list their concerns. They specify a goal.

Ways of working: You may wish to specify a challenge topic – especially if there is one issue of evident concern in the community your school serves. Learners with prior experience of projects to improve the school or community may appreciate less prescription.

Differentiation: Support learners by providing an issue and using closed questions to help them identify concerns, for example 'Is it right that . . . ?' Ask them to identify one practical step as a goal that would improve things. Challenge learners to consider different people's perspectives when listing concerns or proposing actions.

Suggested answers:

For a topic on transport:

We're concerned that the road outside the school is congested.

Our goal is to get more children to walk.

For a topic on food:

We're concerned that the food we eat comes from far away and that is not sustainable.

Our goal is to encourage children to eat local food.

For a topic on energy:

We're concerned that we use too much energy in school.

Our goal is to make sure the air con is turned off when it is not needed.

For a topic on keeping safe:

We're concerned that some children go on websites that are not suitable.

Our goal is to make sure all children know the e-safety code.

Main activity (approx. 20–25 mins)

Good for: Applying their understanding of evaluating Zara's resources and applying them to their own topic.

Activity: Having reminded themselves of what it is that they want to change (and how they will recognise sucesss) learners choose their most useful source and evaluate its usefulness in helping them to achieve the goal identified.

Ways of working: Learners with prior experience of evaluating texts could well be confident in using the sentence starters provided to work independently. Learners with less prior experience could use the suggested answers and apply their understanding of this to their own issue.

Differentiation: Support learners by asking closed questions (e.g. 'Does it give facts?', 'Is it about your topic?') Encourage them to look back at their work in the last lesson. Ensure they are clear about their goal. Challenge learners to identify techniques (e.g. of persuasion) in sources unrelated to their topic/goal.

Suggested answers:

For the healthy eating topic:

The most useful source we have found so far is *101 Healthy Recipes*.

There are several reasons for this; firstly, it is designed so that you can use fresh and nutritious ingredients.

In addition, there are clear instructions we can follow.

Furthermore, it tells you which recipes are easy and which ones are hard.

Finally, it gives you an idea about how long it takes to prepare the food/drink.

However, this source still has limitations. The first of these is that it doesn't tell you how to persuade people to try new food.

Also, we don't know how much it will cost to make.

So we will need to find additional sources to help us budget, and how to make our class want to try new things.

For the transport topic:

The most useful source we have found so far is the website of a school with a travel plan.

There are several reasons for this; firstly, it showed you how to plan safe routes to school.

In addition, it showed how they have encouraged more children to walk and cycle.

Furthermore, it tells you how they got some money for building bike storage.

Finally, it gives you an idea about how they encourage parents not to drive children to school.

However, this source still has limitations. The first of these is that it doesn't tell you how to persuade children to change.

Also, we don't know how busy the traffic is around their school. So we will need to find additional sources to help us make a plan suitable for our area.

Peer feedback (approx. 5–10 mins)

Pair each learner with a partner from a different group. Ask them to read each other's evaluations.

- Have they identified relevant uses?
- Have they identified relevant limitations?
- Can they identify additional uses? Limitations?

NB ensure that learners are clear they need to give feedback on skills developed in this lesson – the risk is that they will comment on other skills, for example 'neat handwriting'.

Taking it further: Lessons 1–2

Zara's attempts to persuade her class to try new healthy food could be used a stimulus for a range of structured practical food technology activities. Learners could be challenged to conduct research and analyse the properties of ingredients and consider their appropriateness for a healthy-eating project brief. Catering professionals in the community the school serves could be utilised as potential source of expertise and to further promote engagement.

Developing evaluation skills: Lesson 3

In Lesson 3, learners focus on developing their evaluation of source skills and move on to evaluating arguments. They are introduced to the idea that persuading people to make a positive change can be achieved through using facts and changing people's perspectives.

CAMBRIDGE STAGE 6 EVALUATION LEARNING OBJECTIVES

3.1 Evaluating sources: Discuss a source, considering the author and/or purpose, and comment on its strengths and limitations

3.2 Evaluating arguments: Express opinions about a source, making reference to its features and arguments

LESSON LEARNING GOALS

To develop my knowledge and understanding about:

* how to say what the main viewpoint of a source is

* how to locate words/phrases from a source that could be useful.

Resources needed

Learner's Skills Book 6

Downloadables 3.3, 3.4 and 3.5

Challenge topic (e.g. Keeping healthy)

Highlighters and coloured pens

For challenge: Challenge topic opinion pieces with similar features to the download

Prior learning (approx. 5–10 mins)

Good for: Exploring pupils' attitudes at this stage in their learning.

Activity: Learners are asked to say which of two contrasting opinions most closely reflects their own.

Ways of working: Give learners a minute to silently reflect on their own stance; they can then share ideas in the class discussion. Learners have the opportunity to express a range of perspectives on the issue, depending on the extent to which they take the view that the healthy eating is best promoted by incentivising healthy choices – or by compulsion. Look for learners' evidence and reasoning. Challenge them to articulate how they would convince a sceptic by asking them 'what would you say to someone who . . . ?'.

Differentiation: Support learners by encouraging them to reflect on their own experiences: What experiences have they had of something being banned? Did it work? What experiences have they had of something being incentivised? Did it work? Why? Why not? Challenge learners by asking them to develop their answers (e.g. 'What experiences have led you to come to this conclusion?', 'We could go deeper still – what does this tell us about human nature?')

Suggested answers: This will depend on the learners' experiences and beliefs but look for answers that draw on their own experiences appropriately to make a broader point. For example:

Zara is right because people will never change unless they want to. Our class worked hard to win the attendance prize.

Arun is right because unhealthy food is so popular. Children love sugary drinks so they won't choose healthy ones when they have the choice to still drink what they like.

Starter activity (approx. 10–15 mins)

Good for: Building on prior understanding of text types and applying this to a Global Perspectives context.

Activity: Read through the learning goals for this lesson with learners at the beginning of this activity. Learners decide whether a series of texts are useful because they have facts or different perspectives.

Ways of working: Learners can work individually or in pairs for discussion. Encourage learners to record their own decision even if it differs from their partner's.

Differentiation: Support learners by showing them examples they have previously studied in language lessons. Challenge learners to provide further examples relevant to their own challenge topic.

Suggested answers: See Downloadable 3.3 for a Worked Example of the table.

Main activity (approx. 20–25 mins)

Good for: Learners to develop an understanding of how to approach a text which has a clear perspective on one side of an argument.

Activity: Working from Downloadable 3.4, learners pick out the main ideas (yellow highlighting is suggested) and phrases that could be used in a campaign to promote healthy eating (green highlighting).

Ways of working: This would be a good activity to focus teacher input on a small group with lower prior attainment while those who have higher attainment work independently. Model the opening paragraph using a whiteboard. Encourage learners to use prior understanding of summarising texts. If their experience of this is more limited, spend more time modelling using the Worked Example.

Differentiation: Support learners by working in a small group. Challenge learners to draft the first paragraph of an opinion piece for their challenge topic.

Suggested answers: A Worked Example for the activity is provided as Downloadable 3.5. Suggested responses for the class discussion are:

1   Parents should not send unhealthy food to children's parties.

2   Global statistics are used to establish the extent of the problem. The author appeals to empathy (for the teachers). Causes and consequences of the issue are clear.

3   The opposing case is only briefly considered. We are left thinking more could be said. As a result the conclusion is open to question.

4   Some useful phrases to give a perspective emphasis, for example 'this is outrageous' and the use of rhetorical questions to involve the reader directly.

Developing evaluation skills: Lesson 4

In Lesson 4, learners focus on developing their understanding of different sources. They consider a range of sources, most of them rooted in a particular perspective and consider what kinds of sources could be used to justify their proposed action. They then compare what different sources say about a topic and evaluate the arguments given.

CAMBRIDGE STAGE 6 EVALUATION LEARNING OBJECTIVES

3.1   Evaluating sources: Discuss a source, considering the author and/or purpose, and comment on its strengths and limitations

3.2   Evaluating arguments: Express opinions about a source, making reference to its features and arguments

LESSON LEARNING GOALS

To develop my knowledge and understanding about:

- reasons for choosing a source
- comparing the features of different sources
- comparing what different sources say about a topic.

Resources needed

Learner's Skills Book 6

Downloadables 3.6, 3.7, 3.8 and 3.9

Challenge topic (e.g. Keeping healthy)

If possible, a range of sources relevant to the issue you are working on. Collecting these could be set as a homework activity before the lesson.

Different coloured highlighters

Prior learning (approx. 5–10 mins)

Good for: Assessing learners' prior understanding of relevance.

Activity: Learners match a range of sources to the person who might find them useful based on their goal.

Ways of working: Learners work independently on this activity.

Differentiation: Support learners by encouraging them to look for the most obvious first. They don't have to do them in a particular order. Encourage them to rule out ones that are obviously irrelevant, for example Zara would not need anything about computer hacking. Challenge learners to apply this understanding to their action – what kind of articles, leaflets, surveys could they look for?

Suggested answers: Zara: 1, 4, 9; Arun: 5, 7, 8; Sofia 2, 3, 6

Starter activity (approx. 10–15 mins)

Good for: Learners to identify an issue and different perspectives on it within a source.

Activity: Read through the learning goals for this lesson with learners at the beginning of this activity. Learners are asked to annotate the article in Downloadable 3.6 to locate key ideas, for example, 'what is the problem?'. They identify opposing perspectives using different coloured highlighting.

Ways of working: The article could be distributed to individual learners as a download or put on a whiteboard and annotated/highlighted together as a class activity. Or set as a timed challenge with learners asked to report back. Allow time for learners to share ideas in a class discussion.

Differentiation: Support learners by projecting the text so that you can model how to navigate it. Challenge learners to move quickly on to the extra challenge question. Challenge them further by asking them to highlight sentences in a different colour that someone who is against Sofia's idea could use.

Suggested answers: See Downloadable 3.7 for a Worked Example.

Main activity (approx. 20–25 mins)

Good for: Learners to evaluate a range of sources on one topic; identifying different perspectives.

Activity: Working from the download in Downloadable 3.8, learners identify Purpose, Viewpoint, Author, Strengths and Limitations.

Ways of working: This could be done individually, or the class could initially be divided into four groups. Each group could be allocated a different source. They could report to the class.

For the class discussion, having seen a range of sources, learners consider what they could look for that would be relevant to their topic. Alternatively, they could evaluate sources that they have brought into the lesson. Give them time to reflect on this first for themselves before sharing ideas with the class.

Differentiation: Support learners by encouraging them to identify if the source is 'for' 'against' or 'neutral'. Challenge learners to evaluate the use of language that helped them decide that a source was strongly in support of a particular perspective. To what extent is it persuasive?

Suggested answers: See the Worked Example in Downloadable 3.9. Source C would be most useful to Sofia because it contains parents' direct experiences of the problem. It gives a number of negative consequences.

Peer feedback (approx. 5 mins)

Pair each learner with a partner from a different group. Ask them to give feedback about what sources they think would help to justify their action.

Taking it further: Lessons 3–4

Encourage learners to investigate a historical example of a campaign for change. As an outcome of this enquiry, learners could be challenged to produce structured accounts including support from a range of evidence. This process can be used to develop their understanding of the way historians make use of a range of different sources in order to reach conclusions. As learners explore different accounts they can be given opportunities to identify and explain different ways in which the campaign for change was viewed at the time – and subsequently.

Getting better at evaluation skills: Lesson 5

In Lesson 5, learners focus on getting better at evaluating sources, by thinking about how a source can be chosen to support a course of action, and evaluating arguments, by comparing sources according to their features and viewpoints.

CAMBRIDGE STAGE 6 EVALUATION LEARNING OBJECTIVES

3.1 Evaluating sources: Discuss a source, considering the author and/or purpose, and comment on its strengths and limitations

3.2 Evaluating arguments: Express opinions about a source, making reference to its features and arguments

LESSON LEARNING GOALS

To get better at:

- giving my reasons for choosing a source
- comparing the features and viewpoints of different sources.

Resources needed

Learner's Skills Book 6

Downloadables 3.10 and 3.11

Challenge topic (e.g. Reduce, re-use, recycle)

Sources on local issues if Downloadable 3.10 is not being used for all learners (see Main activity).

Prior learning (approx. 5–10 mins)

Good for: Building on previous knowledge.

Activity: Ask learners to look at a list of sources and decide which would be most useful to support a course of action.

Ways of working: Learners can work individually on the task to begin with before getting into pairs or small groups to discuss their work. Stage a plenary session to give learners the opportunity to share their ideas and respond to others.

Differentiation: Support learners by checking their understanding of the different types of source in the list by using questioning. Challenge learners to explain why they think a source will be useful (or why other sources would not be useful).

Suggested answers: Accept any reasonable choice of two sources, especially those supported by evidence or reasoning.

a could be used as evidence of the pressure young people are under to buy plastic

b could be used as evidence of the impact of plastic pollution on the local community

c could support the idea that action needs to be taken to deal with the problem of plastic

d could give practical information about setting up a recycling point

e could provide evidence of the long-term effects of plastic pollution globally

f could support the idea that local people are increasingly concerned about the environment.

Starter activity (approx. 10–15 mins)

Good for: Getting better at identifying sources that could be used to support a course of action to solve a local problem, giving reasons.

Activity: Read through the learning goals for this lesson with learners at the beginning of this activity. Ask learners to think of a course of action that they could take to solve a local problem, and consider what sources they could use to support it. They then consider different ways in which sources can be useful in supporting an action.

Ways of working: Learners work in small groups to select a local issue they would like to take action on and discuss what sources would be useful to support that action.

Differentiation: Support learners by helping them to decide on a local problem of interest to them, or by providing a topic for them to focus on. Suggest a number of different sources they could use. Challenge learners to come up with their own local issue and to decide on a course of action. Encourage learners to think of a range of local sources that could be useful in supporting their action.

Suggested answers:

Responses to the first two questions will depend to some extent on the local problems identified by the groups.

It might be helpful to remind learners of the difference between primary and secondary sources and the fact that a source doesn't have to be a written text but could include radio/TV broadcasts, video, and so on.

Accept any reasonable responses, especially those supported by evidence or reasoning.

For the class discussion, sources could be useful, for example, if they:

- present arguments justifying a course of action
- provide evidence (facts, statistics, etc.) to support an argument
- give examples/experiences of similar actions carried out by others
- offer practical advice/tips on how to carry out an action.

However, to be really effective in any of these ways, a source should also be reliable, not unduly biased or opinion-based, and so on. This will need to be judged according to where and when the source comes from (does it come from an organisation or outlet with a reputation for reliability? Is it up-to-date?), who the author is (do they have any expertise in the subject?), what the purpose of the source is (does it present just one side of an argument?), and so on.

Main activity (approx. 20–25 mins)

Good for: Getting better at comparing different sources according to their features and their viewpoints.

Activity: Ask learners either to compare two sources on a local problem of their own choice, or to compare two sources provided by the teacher (Downloadable 3.10), in terms of their features and their viewpoints, before deciding which would be most useful in support of an action.

Ways of working: Learners work in small groups. If you are using the sources provided, some groups can be given Source A to work on and others can be given Source B. Learners can then be paired from different groups to exchange information about their source. Stage a plenary session at the end of the activity, giving learners the opportunity to share their ideas and respond to others.

Differentiation: Support learners by providing them with only one source to work with (A or B) and then pair them with a learner who has worked on the other source. They then exchange information about their source in order to complete the table. Challenge learners to work with two sources and to reach a decision about which source is most useful to support their action.

Suggested answers:

See Downloadable 3.11. Responses to the follow-on question might be:

Source A because it describes a service for plastic recycling that the school could use.

Source B because it explains how to make recycling plastic more effective and other things we can do to reduce plastic pollution.

Taking it further: Lesson 5

If learners have focused on an issue of their own choice in this lesson, encourage them to investigate a range of sources relating to this issue and to make a display of the sources they have found most useful. This could include screenshots of useful websites or videos, examples of printed matter such as leaflets, newspapers, advertisements, and so on. They could annotate the sources, highlighting their features and viewpoints.

If learners have focused on the issue of plastic recycling using the sources provided in Lesson 5, encourage them to find other local sources about recycling, and to create a similar display. They could use these sources to investigate recycling facilities in their local area, for example by creating a map of where such facilities are located and what services they provide. Alternatively, invite someone who is involved in a local recycling scheme to visit the class and answer questions on the topic. Challenge learners to come up with ways of promoting the message of 'Reduce, re-use, recycle' among their peers or a wider audience, by scripting and performing dramatic sketches, creating songs or jingles, designing posters and signs, and so on.

> Reflection

SKILLS SECTION	CROSS-CURRICULAR LINKS *Learners have opportunities to apply their knowledge and understanding of, and skills in:*	TOPICS MODELLED
Starting with	Science: thinking and working scientifically • Sort, group and classify objects, materials and living things through testing, observation and using secondary information Geography: physical geography • Water cycle, biomes Geography: human geography • Economic activity, distribution of natural resources History: • Understanding evidence and different interpretations of the past Language skills: reading • Express personal responses to texts, including preferences in terms of language, style and themes	Reduce, re-use, recycle Sharing Planet Earth
Developing	Science: science in context • Use science to support points when discussing issues, situations or actions • Discuss how the use of science and technology can have positive and negative environmental effects on their local area Geography: human geography • Economic activity, distribution of natural resources Art and design: • Thinking and working artistically Language skills: speaking and listening • Listen, reflect on what is heard, and give a reasoned response with reference to at least one specific point made by the speaker • Structure information to aid the listener's understanding of the main and subsidiary points Science: science in context • Use science to support points when discussing issues, situations or actions • Discuss how the use of science and technology can have positive and negative environmental effects on their local area	Sharing Planet Earth Water, food and farming

SKILLS SECTION	CROSS-CURRICULAR LINKS *Learners have opportunities to apply their knowledge and understanding of, and skills in:*	TOPICS MODELLED
Getting better at	Science: science in context • Use science to support points when discussing issues, situations or actions • Discuss how the use of science and technology can have positive and negative environmental effects on their local area Geography: human geography • Economic activity, distribution of natural resources PE: • analysing and evaluating group/ team performance with reference to technique and/or tactics	Sharing Planet Earth Keeping healthy Moving goods and people

The cross-curricular links in this table are reproduced from Cambridge International curriculum frameworks. This Cambridge International copyright material is reproduced under licence and remains the intellectual property of Cambridge Assessment International Education.

Starting with reflection skills: Lesson 1

In Lesson 1, learners focus on starting to learn about personal viewpoints, by reflecting on what they have learnt and how it affects their thinking on a topic, and on personal learning, by reflecting on the skills used during a team activity and how they can be developed.

CAMBRIDGE STAGE 6 REFLECTION LEARNING OBJECTIVES

4.3 Personal viewpoints: Discuss ways that personal ideas may have been influenced by new information or the ideas of others

4.4 Personal learning: Identify skills learnt or improved during an activity

LESSON LEARNING GOALS

To start to:

• talk about what I have learnt and how my ideas have changed

• talk about a skill that I have got better at.

Resources needed

Learner's Skills Book 6

Downloadable 4.1

Challenge topic (e.g. Reduce, re-use, recycle, Sharing Planet Earth)

Prior learning (approx. 10–15 mins)

Good for: Starting to work effectively as individuals within a team, contributing to the overall team effort.

Activity: Ask learners to evaluate and extract information from the research notes provided in Downloadable 4.1.

Ways of working: Work in groups, ideally with four in a group. Each group member is given a separate set of research notes to work with. Working individually, group members select three facts from the information in their notes and share them with the rest of the group.

Differentiation: Support learners by checking their understanding of the topic (plastic pollution) and the information in the research notes by using questioning. Where appropriate, pair learners to support each other in completing the task. Challenge learners to explain their choice of three facts, especially in terms of how the facts might help to change people's attitude towards plastic.

Suggested answers: There are no definitive answers: the facts chosen will vary from learner to learner. Where possible, ask learners to give reasons for their choice and to respond to choices made by others.

Starter activity (approx. 5–10 mins)

Good for: Building on previous knowledge.

Activity: Read through the learning goals for this lesson with learners at the beginning of this activity. Ask learners to read some short quotations relating to roles during teamwork and to identify which role each quotation refers to.

Ways of working: Learners work individually on the task to begin with before getting into pairs or small groups to discuss their work. Stage a plenary session to check answers with the whole class.

Differentiation: Support learners by checking their understanding of the different roles in a team by using questioning. Challenge learners to explain how they were able to identify which role each quotation refers to and to describe what other roles there can be in a team.

Suggested answers:

Facilitator: Zara; Recorder: Marcus; Reporter: Sofia; Timekeeper: Arun

Responses to the class discussion questions might be:

1   Other roles could include 'Resource manager' (providing everyone with materials they need to complete their tasks), 'Quality checker' (makes sure that everything is accurate and correct), 'Trouble shooter' (deals with problems when they arise), and so on. Names of roles may vary – for example, some might prefer 'Group Leader' to 'Facilitator'.

2   When learners express their individual preferences for a role, ask them to justify their choice. Look for answers that refer to skills that would enhance their ability to carry out the role, for example Facilitator – because I'm good at listening to others and making decisions; Reporter – because I'm good at speaking in public; Recorder – because I'm good at making notes of what people say; Timekeeper – because I'm good at keeping to a timetable, and so on.

Main activity (approx. 20–25 mins)

Good for: Starting to reflect on what has been learnt and how it affects thinking on a topic, and on the skills used during a group activity.

Activity: Ask learners to work in groups. Using their individually compiled lists of three facts about plastic from the Starter activity, learners now reach a group decision on which four facts to choose from those lists in order to compile a single group list. They then reflect

on what they have learnt and on the skills involved in completing the group task.

Ways of working: Learners work in groups, ideally of four. If time allows, groups can report back in a plenary session at the end of the activity. They then work individually to reflect on their learning and the skills they have used.

Differentiation: Support learners by helping them to establish what their roles within the group will be (see the Starter activity). Challenge learners to decide for themselves what these roles will be. Encourage learners to reflect individually on the activities they have carried out.

Suggested answers: The list of 'top four facts' will vary from group to group. Encourage learners to explain their choices, for example when reporting back to the class.

Possible responses might be:

My group's top four facts about plastic:

1   A dead whale has been found with 100 kg of plastic in its stomach.

2   Microplastics are getting into people's food and water.

3   Less than 20 percent of plastic packaging is recycled.

4   Gases from burning plastic cause global warming and harm human health.

Responses to the reflection questions will vary from learner to learner. Based on the example answers above, possible responses are:

1   Up to 50 percent of plastic items are used only once and then thrown away.

2   We need to make more things from materials other than plastic, such as paper, glass or metal, which can be recycled.

3   I'll try to avoid using single-use plastic, such as fizzy drinks bottles, and get a re-usable water bottle instead.

4   I worked well with my teammates and communicated with them, and then I reflected on what we did.

5   I'm better at communicating now because I listen more carefully to what my teammates say.

6   I'd like to improve my teamwork by making more useful suggestions about how to do things.

Encourage learners to understand the difference

between learning a fact (e.g. only 20 percent of plastic packaging is recycled) and how this affects their way of thinking about a topic (e.g. to reduce plastic waste, we need to use alternative materials that can be recycled or are biodegradable).

Possible answers to the class discussion questions:

1   There are no definitive answers. Accept any reasonable responses, especially if supported by evidence and reasoning. Encourage learners to say why they think a particular skill is important in the context of teamwork. Learners are likely to include the skills of collaboration (for example, when planning and dividing tasks, or when working

together to solve problems) and communication (for example, when presenting information, and when listening to one another), but may also refer to analysis (for example, when analysing a task to see what needs to be done, so that roles and tasks can be assigned within the group).

2   This might be a good opportunity to emphasise the importance of reflection skills in the context of teamwork (for example, when reflecting on strengths and limitations of personal contribution, on the benefits and challenges of working as a team, or on what other skills have been developed through teamwork).

Starting with reflection skills: Lesson 2

In Lesson 2, learners focus on starting to learn about Personal contribution, by reflecting on an example of teamwork that they have engaged in, and on teamwork, by reflecting on positive and negative aspects of their experience.

CAMBRIDGE STAGE 6 REFLECTION LEARNING OBJECTIVES

4.1   Personal contribution: Discuss the impact of personal contribution to teamwork

4.2   Teamwork: Identify benefits and challenges of working together to achieve a shared outcome

LESSON LEARNING GOALS

To start to:

*   talk about what I did as a member of my team

*   talk about positive or negative experiences when working as a member of a team.

Resources needed

Learner's Skills Book 6

Downloadable 4.2

Challenge topic (e.g. Reduce, re-use, recycle, Sharing Planet Earth)

Prior learning (approx. 5–10 mins)

Good for: Building on previous knowledge.

Activity: Ask learners to read a short text and answer two questions about it.

Ways of working: Learners work on the task individually to begin with before getting into pairs or small groups to discuss their work.

Differentiation: Support learners by checking their understanding of the text by using questioning. Challenge learners to explain their answers and to consider what action could be taken.

Suggested answers:

1   **b** an environmental campaigner

2   **d** to persuade people to use less plastic

Starter activity (approx. 10–15 mins)

Good for: Starting to prepare learners for a teamwork activity by considering their personal perspective on a global issue.

Activity: Read through the learning goals for this lesson with learners at the beginning of this activity. Ask learners to rank a list of items according to their personal experience of using the items in their everyday lives.

Ways of working: Learners work individually before getting into pairs or small groups to discuss their work.

Differentiation: Support learners by checking their understanding of the items in the list by using questioning. Challenge learners to explain how they have ranked the items and to come up with ways that people could use less plastic.

Suggested answers: Ranking of the items will depend on individual learners' own personal experiences. For the class discussion questions, learners can draw on information from the previous lesson:

1   Encourage answers ranging from the items being recycled or re-used to their being put into landfill, incinerated or becoming litter or pollution in the environment.

2   Encourage answers that recognise that most plastic waste is not biodegradable, so if it isn't recycled or re-used (or destroyed by incineration, which creates harmful gases), it lingers in the environment, gradually being worn down into smaller and smaller particles (microplastics) that eventually enter the food chain and the water supply.

3   Encourage answers that recognise the importance of recycling and re-using but also acknowledge that they are limited in effectiveness. Over the long term, reducing or avoiding altogether the use of plastics, or replacing them with alternative materials that are recyclable and/or biodegradable, will provide more sustainable solutions.

Main activity (approx. 20–25 mins)

Good for: Starting to reflect on personal contribution to the work of the team and on positive and negative aspects of teamwork.

Activity: Ask learners to read a short dialogue about the problem of plastic and then to work in teams to identify actions that could be taken with regard to four of the single-use plastic items in the list. Having completed this task, learners give each other peer feedback on their contributions to the team effort and reflect on positive and negative aspects of their experience.

Ways of working: Learners work in groups initially and then reflect individually on their own and others' contributions to the team effort before sharing their

ideas as peer feedback. They then have the opportunity in a class discussion to reflect more generally on personal contribution and teamwork.

Differentiation: Support learners by helping them to establish useful roles in the group so that all members make a contribution. Challenge learners to decide on their roles themselves and to complete the team task independently as a group.

Suggested answers: Items chosen will vary from group to group. See Downloadable 4.2 for a Worked Example.

For the class discussion questions:

Responses will vary according to learners' personal experiences of teamwork. Look for responses that show an awareness of what all team members should be doing, for example communicating well with each other; knowing what their individual role involves, what tasks they have to complete, and by when; respecting other team members' opinions; helping each other to complete tasks; acknowledging their own personal strengths.

Encourage learners to base their responses on their recent experiences of teamwork, and to identify specific areas for improvement. Challenge them to come up with practical ideas as to how the improvements can be achieved.

Peer feedback (approx. 5–10 mins)

Begin peer feedback by giving each learner the opportunity to reflect individually on their personal contribution to the teamwork activity they have just carried out, and on the contributions of others, using the table. They then share their ideas with the others in their group as a way of enabling each learner to identify their most helpful personal contribution. This will vary from learner to learner, but they should be encouraged to focus only on positive contributions. Finally, encourage learners to reflect more generally on advantages (e.g. sharing of ideas and workload, potentially shortening the time it takes to complete the task, etc.) and disadvantages (e.g. having to resolve disagreements, etc.) of working as a team.

Starting with reflection skills: Lesson 3

In Lesson 3, learners focus on starting to learn about personal contribution, teamwork, personal viewpoints and personal learning, by taking part in a teamwork activity and then reflecting on their experience of working as a team to achieve a task.

CAMBRIDGE STAGE 6 REFLECTION LEARNING OBJECTIVES

4.1 Personal contribution: Discuss the impact of personal contribution to teamwork

4.2 Teamwork: Identify benefits and challenges of working together to achieve a shared outcome

4.3 Personal viewpoints: Discuss ways that personal ideas may have been influenced by new information or the ideas of others

4.4 Personal learning: Identify skills learnt or improved during an activity

LESSON LEARNING GOALS

To start to:

- talk about what I did as a member of my team

- talk about positive or negative experiences when working as a member of a team

- talk about what I have learnt and how my ideas have changed

- talk about a skill that I have got better at.

Resources needed

Learner's Skills Book 6

Downloadable 4.3

Challenge topic (e.g. Reduce, re-use, recycle, Sharing Planet Earth)

Sheets of blank A4 paper and felt pens (or preferred method of planning slides)

Prior learning (approx. 5–10 mins)

Good for: Building on previous knowledge.

Activity: Ask learners to read some short statements by learners and to identify what skills they are reflecting on.

Ways of working: Learners work individually on the task to begin with before getting into pairs or small groups to discuss their work. Stage a plenary session to check answers with the whole class.

Differentiation: Support learners by checking their understanding of the skills listed by using questioning. Challenge learners to explain how they matched the statements and skills.

Suggested answers: Research: Zara; Analysis: Arun; Evaluation: Marcus; Reflection: Sofia.

First activity (approx. 20–25 mins)

Good for: Starting to work as a group in order to organise how a task is carried out.

Activity: Read through the learning goals for this lesson with learners at the beginning of this activity. Ask the learners to work in groups to prepare a team presentation for a particular purpose and audience by planning the content of two slides. They can draw on ideas and information from the previous two lessons in order to do this.

Ways of working: Learners work in groups, ideally with four in a group. Setting a deadline for completion will encourage groups to organise the work efficiently among themselves. Groups give feedback on their work in the class discussion.

Differentiation: Support learners by establishing useful roles within the group and allocating tasks. Challenge learners to decide for themselves what roles are needed and to divide the work among members of the group so that everyone makes a contribution.

Suggested answers: The content of the slides will vary from group to group. Encourage learners to think of combining powerful images and important information in the design of their slides.

For the class discussion questions, encourage learners to reflect on the process of carrying out the activity as a team:

1   What roles were needed? How was the work divided up among the group members?

2   Were roles clearly defined and tasks allocated fairly? Were there any conflicts within the group that needed resolution?

3   How did members of the group monitor one another's progress? How did they help one another to complete tasks?

Second activity (approx. 10–15 mins)

Good for: Starting to reflect on the experience of working as a team.

Activity: Ask learners to reflect on the teamwork they have just carried out by answering a series of questions.

Ways of working: Learners work with a partner (preferably from a different group). They discuss and record their responses to a series of prompts asking them to reflect on the experience of working as a team.

Differentiation: Support learners by selecting a few of the prompts for them to discuss with a partner. Challenge learners to discuss and respond to all the prompts in order to reflect on teamwork. Encourage learners to look for similarities and differences between their own and their partner's experience of working as a team.

Suggested answers: See the Worked Example in Downloadable 4.3.

Taking it further: Lessons 1–3

What makes teamwork successful? When learners have identified useful team roles (facilitator, recorder, etc.) ask them to create a display describing what each role involves. This could then be put up in the classroom and referred to when establishing or clarifying roles in future teamwork activities. It could be supplemented by creating a list of 'DOs and DON'Ts' for successful teamwork, drawn from the learners' own experience. In addition, create a bank of useful things to say when working as a team, which could contain examples of giving praise and encouragement, asking for clarification, giving reminders, offering advice, making suggestions, and so on. This could also be displayed in the classroom for future reference during teamwork activities.

Developing reflection skills: Lesson 4

In Lesson 4, learners focus on developing their personal contribution, by working together in order to achieve a shared goal, and on teamwork, by reflecting on their personal experience of working as a team.

CAMBRIDGE STAGE 6 REFLECTION LEARNING OBJECTIVES

4.1   Personal contribution: Discuss the impact of personal contribution to teamwork

4.2   Teamwork: Identify benefits and challenges of working together to achieve a shared outcome

LESSON LEARNING GOALS

To develop my knowledge and understanding about:

- how to talk about what I did as a member of my team

- how to talk about positive or negative experiences when working as a member of a team.

Resources needed

Learner's Skills Book 6

Downloadables 4.4, 4.5 and 4.6

Challenge topic (e.g. Sharing Planet Earth, Water, food and farming)

Prior learning (approx. 5–10 mins)

Good for: Building on previous knowledge.

Activity: Ask learners to match some short texts to their sources.

Ways of working: Learners can work on the task individually to begin with before getting into pairs or small groups to discuss their work. Stage a plenary session to check answers with the whole class.

Differentiation: Support learners by checking their understanding of the texts and the sources by using questioning and/or by limiting the number of texts you ask them to work with. Challenge learners to explain why they have identified a text as belonging to a particular source and to explain why they think some sources are more reliable than others.

Suggested answers: 1 = Source C; 2 = Source A; 3 = Source D; 4 = Source E; 5 = Source B

The more reliable sources are likely to be the biology textbook and the newspaper article: the former because the writer probably has a good level of expertise and because of the editing process it has been through; the latter again because it has probably been reviewed and edited by more than one person.

First activity (approx. 20–25 mins)

Good for: Developing learners' experience of working as a member of a team to achieve a shared outcome.

Activity: Read through the learning goals for this lesson with learners at the beginning of this activity. Ask learners to share information from their notes with one another in their group, making their own notes in a grid of the information they need in order to answer the questions.

Ways of working: Learners work in groups, ideally with four in each group. Give each learner a different set of notes (A–D) from Downloadable 4.4. Where this isn't possible, either assign one set of notes to be shared by two learners (i.e. where the group size is bigger than four) or assign two sets to the same learner (i.e. where the group size is smaller than four). Stress to learners that they don't need to understand everything in the notes you give them, but they should focus on finding and noting down only the information that is relevant to answering the questions on the grid. Encourage learners to share information from their notes orally rather than showing it to the others. This will encourage them to listen to one another and ensure that all group members

participate in the activity. All learners make notes in the grid provided in Downloadable 4.5 of the information shared within the group in order to answer the questions. Set a time limit for the information-sharing activity (e.g. 10 minutes), as this will encourage learners to focus on selecting the most useful information from their notes and to write concisely rather than at length.

Differentiation: Support learners by checking their understanding of the content of the set of notes they are given by using questioning. Alternatively, pair learners so that two learners work with the same set of notes. Challenge learners to be selective in the information they share with the group, focusing on the information from their notes most relevant to answering the questions rather than reading out the whole text.

Suggested answers: For the class discussion, no prior knowledge of the topic is expected; learners can talk from personal experience or their own general knowledge. Encourage learners to start asking their own questions about the topic.

Downloadable 4.6 provides an example of how a completed grid might look.

Second activity (approx. 10–15 mins)

Good for: Developing learners' ability to reflect on the experience of working as a member of a team, its benefits and challenges.

Activity: Ask learners to reflect and make notes on the experience of working as a team to complete the Starter activity.

Ways of working: Learners work on the task individually to begin with before getting into pairs to discuss their work. Stage a plenary session to encourage learners to think about teamwork in general, based on their personal experience of it.

Differentiation: Support learners by encouraging them to talk about their personal experiences as a member of a team trying to achieve a shared goal in the Starter activity. Challenge learners to make generalised statements about teamwork, supported by evidence and reasoning.

Suggested answers: There are no definitive answers to the questions for reflection, as the experience of the Starter activity will vary from individual to individual. Examples of responses include:

1   a   I listened carefully when others were speaking and made notes of what they said.

b I found the most useful information in my source and shared it with others.

c I decided who in our group would speak first, second, and so on, and for how long.

d I asked questions if I didn't understand something.

2 a I could have listened more carefully to what others said.

b I could have read my source more carefully, and found more useful information.

c I could have helped to organise our group so we worked more efficiently.

d I could have asked questions if I didn't understand something.

3 a Working as a team made it easier, because we

shared the work and did it more quickly.

b Working as a team made it harder, because we couldn't agree how to organise the work.

4 a Teamwork is better when someone makes decisions about how to organise the work.

b Teamwork is better when everyone does their fair share of the work.

c Teamwork means information can be shared more quickly.

d Teamwork means listening to others even when you don't agree with them.

For the class discussion, encourage learners to draw general conclusions about teamwork from their experiences, rather than just focusing on particular examples of benefits or challenges.

Developing reflection skills: Lesson 5

In Lesson 5, learners focus on developing their personal viewpoints, by reflecting on what they have learnt from their experience of working as a team; and personal learning, by reflecting on the skills they have developed as a result of working as a team.

CAMBRIDGE STAGE 6 REFLECTION LEARNING OBJECTIVES

4.3 Personal viewpoints: Discuss ways that personal ideas may have been influenced by new information or the ideas of others

4.4 Personal learning: Identify skills learnt or improved during an activity

LESSON LEARNING GOALS

To develop my knowledge and understanding of:

- how to talk about what I have learnt and how my ideas have changed
- how to talk about a skill that I have got better at.

Resources needed

Learner's Skills Book 6

Downloadables 4.7 and 4.8

Challenge topic (e.g. Sharing Planet Earth, Water, food and farming)

Prior learning (approx. 5–10 mins)

Good for: Building on previous knowledge.

Activity: Ask learners to read a reflection on a teamwork activity, and answer some questions about it.

Ways of working: Learners can work individually on the task to begin with, before getting into pairs or small groups to discuss their work. Stage a plenary session to get feedback.

Differentiation: Support learners by checking their understanding of the reflection text by using questioning. Challenge learners to find more than one answer to each of the questions.

Suggested answers:

1 Marcus has learnt that bees pollinate crops, that bees are threatened by the use of pesticides and that bees can be helped by growing more plants.

2 Marcus now understands the importance of bees to humans; he understands that people need to help bees.

3 Marcus found out how to help bees; he suggested an action his team could take.

4 Marcus used research skills to find out more about bees, communication skills to listen to other

members of the team and team skills to make a useful suggestion.

Starter activity (approx. 10–15 mins)

Good for: Developing learners' ideas about how a team can plan a course of action in order to achieve a shared goal.

Activity: Read through the learning goals for this lesson with learners at the beginning of this activity. Ask learners to look at a planned course of action (provided in Downloadable 4.7), and to start to consider what decisions have to be made in order for it to be carried out.

Ways of working: Learners should be given the opportunity to discuss the questions for class discussion in pairs or small groups before discussing them in a plenary session. Learners only need to read and discuss the table in Downloadable 4.7 at this point so that their understanding of it can be checked. They complete the table as part of the Main activity.

Differentiation: Support learners by checking their understanding of the table by using questioning (e.g. 'What is the team trying to achieve?', 'Why have they made this table?', 'What do they have to decide?' etc.). Challenge learners to explain how the different tasks in the planned course of action can be divided between the team members and why this needs to be done.

Suggested answers:

1   Encourage learners to come up with ideas such as the need for an eye-catching image, a memorable slogan conveying an important message and information to support that message.

2   Learners can suggest any of the information about bees shared in the previous lesson.

3   The information should in some way support the message of the poster, adding to its persuasive power. (For example, if the slogan is 'Save the Bees!', the information could be about why bees are in danger.)

4   Focus discussion on why different roles should be allocated to different members of the team. In this case, it could be that Marcus has particular skills that he can apply to the task (e.g. he's good at drawing, or he's good at searching for images online). Alternatively, Marcus might have ended up doing this task because others in the team are better at doing some of the other tasks than he is, and so it means that he does his fair share of the work.

5   Focus discussion on the idea that other team members are carrying out different tasks at the same time as Marcus, highlighting the fact that team members can work independently of each other, and yet still be contributing to achieving the team goal. In this case, Sofia, Arun and Zara are probably working on steps 2 and 3 so that everyone can contribute to step 4. (It might also be helpful to point out that some tasks on the list can be done individually, while others can be done by more than one team member.)

Main activity (approx. 20–25 mins)

Good for: Developing learners' ability to plan and organise teamwork so that everyone contributes towards achieving a shared goal.

Activity: Ask the learners to make decisions about how a planned course of action will be carried out, for example by allocating roles within the group, identifying how a task will be completed and setting deadlines for completion. Learners then have the opportunity to reflect on this process and to give peer feedback on how well it has been carried out.

Ways of working: Learners work in small groups, ideally with four in a group. They complete the table provided in Downloadable 4.7 collaboratively and then reflect on the experience in their groups before giving feedback in a class discussion. Each learner should then be paired with a learner from a different group in order to get peer feedback on the decisions they have made.

Differentiation: Support learners by suggesting different roles that can be allocated in each group in order to carry out the work efficiently. For example, in each group there could be one learner who keeps the group 'on track' by allowing a certain amount of time for discussion of each point, while another learner records the group's decisions, and so on. Challenge learners to find solutions to the challenges they face when making decisions (e.g. when not everyone can agree on what to do).

Suggested answers:

For a Worked Example of the table, see Downloadable 4.8.

1   Encourage learners to talk about their experiences of carrying out the Main activity and to share their solutions to overcoming the challenges they faced. Highlight the need to reach compromises when not everyone agrees so that the team can still achieve its goal.

2 'Skills' here is being used loosely, and not strictly in the sense of the skill strands in the Primary Global Perspectives curriculum – although it may be useful to refer to them. For example, learners may have had to analyse the tasks listed in the table in order to understand what each involved, and to evaluate the decisions they made or the arguments put forward in support of each decision. They may have reflected on previous experiences (positive and negative) of teamwork in order to find solutions to challenges and to have used teamwork skills and communication in order to work effectively as a group to achieve their shared goal.

3 Responses will vary from learner to learner. Keep the focus on skills that learners have identified in their responses to question 2. Look for responses that show an awareness of what a particular skill involves, and what steps can be taken to improve it.

4 Responses will vary from learner to learner. The focus can be on how to avoid in future the challenges that have been identified in question 1, for example by identifying roles within the team more clearly, keeping to the plan, making more realistic estimates of the time needed to complete tasks, and so on.

Peer feedback (approx. 5–10 mins)

Pair each learner with a partner from a different group. Where any of the answers to the questions about their plan is 'NO', encourage learners to come up with changes to the plan, perhaps through discussion with their partner.

Developing reflection skills: Lesson 6

In Lesson 6, learners focus on developing their personal contribution, by reflecting on what they did to help their team achieve a shared goal: teamwork, by reflecting on benefits and challenges of working as a team; personal viewpoints, by reflecting on how their thinking has changed as a result of the experience of working as a team; and personal learning, by reflecting on how their experience of teamwork is likely to change the way they do it in future.

CAMBRIDGE STAGE 6 REFLECTION LEARNING OBJECTIVES

4.1 Personal contribution: Discuss the impact of personal contribution to teamwork

4.2 Teamwork: Identify benefits and challenges of working together to achieve a shared outcome

4.3 Personal viewpoints: Discuss ways that personal ideas may have been influenced by new information or the ideas of others

4.4 Personal learning: Identify skills learnt or improved during an activity

LESSON LEARNING GOALS

To develop my knowledge and understanding about:

- how to talk about what I did as a member of my team
- how to talk about positive or negative experiences when working as a member of a team
- how to talk about what I have learnt and how my ideas have changed
- how to talk about a skill that I have got better at.

Resources needed

Learner's Skills Book 6

Challenge topic (e.g. Sharing Planet Earth, Water, food and farming)

Sheets of A4 paper

Team action plan from the previous lesson

Prior learning (approx. 5–10 mins)

Good for: Building on previous knowledge.

Activity: Ask learners to read a short personal reflection text and to identify topics in the text.

Ways of working: Learners work individually on the task before getting into pairs or small groups to discuss their work. Stage a plenary session to check answers with the whole class.

Differentiation: Support learners by checking their understanding of the text by using questioning. Challenge learners to explain how they were able to identify the different topics.

Suggested answers: a = 6 and 9; b = 1, c = 2, 5 and 8; d = 7; e = 3, f = 4.

First activity (approx. 20–25 mins)

Good for: Developing learners' experience of working as part of a team following a planned course of action in order to achieve a shared goal.

Activity: Read through the learning goals for this lesson with learners at the beginning of this activity. Ask learners to complete the design of a poster, following their decisions on how to do this from the previous lesson.

Ways of working: As far as possible, learners work in the same groups as in the previous lesson so that they can follow steps 1–4 of the plan of action that they decided on in that lesson. If time allows at the end of the activity, encourage learners to display their poster designs and get feedback from other groups. Ask learners to identify different elements of a good poster in their finished designs, as listed in the plan (i.e. an eye-catching image, a memorable slogan, information to support the message of the poster).

Differentiation: Support learners by reviewing with them their plan from the previous lesson so that they can identify what they need to do to help their team achieve their shared goal. Challenge learners to achieve the team's shared goal by creating a poster design that all team members have made a contribution to.

Suggested answers: Responses will vary. Encourage learners to stick to their plan from the previous lesson as much as possible and do what they need to do to help their team achieve their shared goal of creating a poster design.

Second activity (approx. 10–15 mins)

Good for: Developing learners' ability to reflect on how the experience of working as a team has changed their thinking and behaviour with regard to teamwork.

Activity: Ask learners to reflect on their experience of working as a team to design a poster, and to think about changes to their thinking and behaviour that have occurred as a result of the experience.

Ways of working: Learners work initially in pairs and then, individually, to reflect on their personal experience of teamwork and changes to their way of thinking about it and the way they do it. Stage a plenary at the end of the activity to encourage learners to talk about what they have learnt from the experience and to draw some general conclusions about teamwork.

Differentiation: Support learners by encouraging them to talk about their personal experience of teamwork before attempting to write about it. This can be done by putting them in pairs with a learner from a different group. Challenge learners to come up with different ways in which their thinking and behaviour has changed as a result of their experience.

Suggested answers: Learners' responses will vary according to their individual experience. They might look like this:

1. a I thought of a memorable slogan for our team's poster.

   b I would help other team members if they couldn't finish their work in time.

2. a Everyone shared their ideas about how to design the best poster.

   b We could ask if other members of the team need help to finish their work.

3. I used to think working as a team wasn't a good way of doing things because everyone wanted to do everything themselves but now I think teamwork is more efficient, because if you make a good plan then everyone knows what they have to do.

4. In the past, when I worked in a team, I used to finish what I had to do and then just play around, but now I check the team's plan to see what else needs to be done and see if anyone needs help.

For the class discussion, accept any reasonable responses, especially responses that are supported by evidence or reasoning. Encourage learners to draw general conclusions rather than focusing on particular incidents that occurred during the lesson. Allow opportunities for learners to respond to what others say.

Taking it further: Lessons 4–6

To reinforce learning about teamwork, groups of learners could be asked to script short dramatic sketches focusing on issues that can arise when working together as a team (e.g. a conflict over deciding who should do what in the team, or dealing with someone who isn't doing what they've been asked to do, etc.). These could be performed in front of the class, who could then discuss solutions to the issues shown in the sketches.

If time allows, give groups of learners the opportunity to execute their design for a poster, as planned in Lesson 6, by carrying out steps 5–7 from Lesson 5. Encourage learners to present their completed posters to the class, allowing each member of the team to give a commentary on the strengths and limitations of their personal contribution to the team's project.

Getting better at reflection skills: Lesson 7

In Lesson 7, learners focus on improving their Personal contribution, by reflecting on their personal contribution; and teamwork, by evaluating benefits and challenges they encountered in working as part of a team.

> ## CAMBRIDGE STAGE 6 REFLECTION LEARNING OBJECTIVES
>
> 4.1 Personal contribution: Discuss the impact of personal contribution to teamwork
>
> 4.2 Teamwork: Identify benefits and challenges of working together to achieve a shared outcome

> ## LESSON LEARNING GOALS
>
> To get better at:
>
> - being clear and talking in a balanced way about what I did as a member of my team
>
> - being clear and talking in a balanced way about positive or negative experiences when working as a member of a team.

Resources needed

Learner's Skills Book 6

Downloadables 4.9, 4.10 and 4.11

Challenge topic (e.g. Sharing Planet Earth, Keeping healthy, Moving goods and people)

Prior learning (approx. 5–10 mins)

Good for: Learners to reflect on their prior experience of teamwork; what conclusions can they reach about the characteristics of effective teams?

Activity: Learners complete the statements 'Good teams always . . . ', 'Good teams never . . . '

Ways of working: Individual reflection in the first instance, followed by paired discussion. Ask if they have identified any common themes? A short class discussion could then ascertain any areas of consensus.

Differentiation: Support learners by providing successful examples of teamwork observed in Lesson 3, reminding them of other opportunities they have had to work in teams across the wider curriculum. Challenge learners to justify why they think their statements hold true generally by providing other examples of teamwork they are familiar with from across the curriculum. Examples could include team sports, or collective ventures studied in other lessons.

Suggested answers: See the Worked Example in Downloadable 4.9.

Starter activity (approx. 10–15 mins)

Good for: Learners to identify different ways in which appropriate reflection can take place following a group action.

Activity: Read through the learning goals for this lesson with learners at the beginning of this activity. Learners read four reflections (provided in Downloadable 4.10) and identify their different successes. After they have finished, they share their assessments in a class discussion.

Ways of working: Learners could work through all of the reflections individually, or they could focus on either Arun, Marcus, Zara or Sofia and then report back to their group.

Differentiation: Support learners by considering individual questions in turn across the four reflections. Challenge learners to explain how each of the reflections could be improved.

Suggested answers: See the Worked Example in Downloadable 4.10.

Main activity (approx. 20–25 mins)

Good for: Applying their understanding of effective reflection (from the starter) to their own action.

Activity: Learners use the sentence starters provided to reflect on an action they have taken. This could be the action in the previous lesson. It would be ideally completed after learners have had prior experience of taking action as a group on an issue of relevance to their locality.

Ways of working: This is designed to provide learners with the opportunity for individual reflection.

Differentiation: Support learners by encouraging them to draw parallels between the action taken and the modelled reflection (in the Starter activity) and their own. What can be used? What needs to be modified? How? Why?

Challenge learners to:

• give specific examples to illustrate the strengths and limitations of their personal contribution to the team

• give a balanced explanation of both the benefits and challenges of working as a team.

Suggested answers:

Possible responses for the bee presentation activity project:

1   The issue we worked on was the crisis in the bee population.

2   This issue is important because we were shocked to find out the damage caused to bees by pesticides. We knew that young children learn about insects and that many parents have gardens.

3   Our goal was to make all of the school aware of the issue.

4   The action we decided to take was to do a presentation to the whole school in assembly.

5   We thought this would be an effective action because we knew that we could get our message to everyone at the same time.

6   My contribution to the team was research on actions that had worked. I was resilient when I found my first results too technical. I was resourceful by getting help from my older sibling who is doing biology.

7   I could have improved my contribution by finding out more about bee-friendly plants that grow in our area.

8   Working as a team helped us to talk to the whole school because we could try it out in the group first.

9   Working as a team was challenging because different people had different ideas, like how to make it simple enough for Stage 1 to understand.

Possible responses for an issue relating to a topic on transport:

1   The issue we worked on was transport to school.

2   This issue is important because the road outside our school is jammed at the start and end of the school day.

3   Our goal was to reduce the number of journeys taken by car.

4   The action we decided to take was to promote 'Walk to school on Wednesday'.

5   We thought this would be an effective action because if we could get children walking on one day a week, they might realise how easy it is.

6   My contribution to the team was collecting the results from each class each Wednesday.

7   I could have improved my contribution by remembering to do it every week.

8   Working as a team helped us to make sure we reached every class in school with posters.

9   Working as a team was challenging because if just two people worked together, the others didn't know what progress had been made. Sometimes that meant we did things twice when we didn't need to.

In evaluating the strengths of their contributions, learners could be encouraged to focus on attributes of successful learners, for example reflectiveness, resourcefulness, resilience, willingness to innovate, flexibility, responsibility.

For the class discussion, advantages and disadvantages of working as part of a team might include:

Advantages	Disadvantages
You can divide up tasks and get the job done more quickly.	Individuals can have less freedom to do things in the way they want to.
You can divide up tasks and work more efficiently.	It is difficult to make a decision – do we have a leader or try to make decisions all together.
People can develop their knowledge/understanding/skills by working alongside others who have prior experience.	It can be harder to change the ideas of a group than an individual.
You can share a sense of success.	Individual members of the group can lose a sense of responsibility – leaving tasks for others.
You get a range of different perspectives to help arrive at a solution – that helps you to be creative.	
As they say, 'the whole is greater than the sum of its parts'. Working as a team opens up new ways of working that the individuals wouldn't have thought of by themselves.	
You can build up a sense of solidarity among the members of the group and they feel like helping each other out.	

Getting better at reflection skills: Lesson 8

In Lesson 8, learners focus on improving their personal viewpoints, by reflecting on ideas that have been changed as a result of an action taken on an issue (their own or one provided); and personal learning, by identifying skills learnt or improved during as a result of this action.

CAMBRIDGE STAGE 6 REFLECTION LEARNING OBJECTIVES

4.3 Personal viewpoints: Discuss ways that personal ideas may have been influenced by new information or the ideas of others

4.4 Personal learning: Identify skills learnt or improved during an activity

LESSON LEARNING GOALS

To get better at:

- talking about how new information or the ideas of others have changed the way I think about a topic

- talking about what skills I have got better at and how.

Resources needed

Learner's Skills Book 6

Downloadables 4.12 and 4.13

Challenge topic (e.g. Sharing Planet Earth, Keeping healthy, Moving goods and people)

Prior learning (approx. 5 mins)

Good for: Activating prior knowledge of planning an action to meet a specified goal, stimulating thought about how this process can develop new skills and/or refine existing ones.

Activity: Learners recall Marcus, Sofia, Arun and Zara's project about the importance of bees. They recall whose ideas they wanted to change and what ideas they wanted to change. They are asked about their goal and are requested to speculate what skills they think were developed in the process.

Ways of working: Learners are asked to note ideas ready for a class discussion. This could be done on whiteboards with each question tackled in turn.

Differentiation: Support learners by a process of questioning that begins with factual questions (e.g. 'What was your topic about?', 'What did you do?') to higher level questioning (e.g. 'Why did you decide to take action on this issue?', 'What did you hope to achieve?') Challenge learners to evaluate the group's action. Was their goal appropriate? How could they have measured their success?

Suggested answers:

1   Children in their school.

2   Perceptions of bees' importance to the ecosystem.

3   To raise awareness.

4   Presentation skills (visual/aural), meeting deadlines, delegating tasks.

Starter activity (approx. 10–15 mins)

Good for: Learners to understand different aspects of reflection that are appropriate when evaluating the success of an action.

Activity: Read through the learning goals for this lesson with learners at the beginning of this activity. Learners read four reflections (provided in Downloadable 4.12) and identify what has been reflected on, and how well.

Ways of working: Learners work individually to fill in the table in the Learner's Skills Book

Differentiation: Support learners by asking them to put a tick (✓) first in the table next to the aspects they think have been explained. Go through one as a group if the process is not clear in the first instance. Challenge learners to suggest how each of the four reflections could have been improved.

Suggested answers: For a Worked Example, see Downloadable 4.13.

Main activity (approx. 20–25 mins)

Good for: Learners to apply their understanding of different aspects of reflection.

Activity: Learners either:

a   imagine they are one of the team in the Starter activity and improve upon their reflection

Or

b   reflect upon an action they have taken.

Ways of working: This is an individual activity.

Differentiation: Support learners by a process of questioning that begins with factual level questioning (e.g. 'What was your issue?', 'What did you do?') to higher level questioning (e.g. 'What did you think at first?', 'What do you think now?', 'What has changed?', 'What caused this change?') Challenge learners to ensure

that the connections between thoughts, behaviour and actions taken are both clear (supported by specific and relevant examples) and well explained (cause/effect follow).

Suggested answers: Responses might look as follows:

The topic I am working on today is Sharing Planet Earth.

1   Before, I used to think that it was just rich countries that had problems with plastic.

I now realise that this is a global problem.

This is because plastic is a cheap material used all around the world.

2   Before, I used to use single-use plastic bags.

However, now I try to re-use cloth bags.

This is because I now know about the great Pacific garbage patch.

3   Before, I used to not be able to sew.

However, now I can do simple stitching.

This is because I needed to sew handles on our bags.

4   Before, I noticed that some learners used to use plastic bags for lunch.

However, now I notice that some are using our bags.

This is because we made some and sold them at the Open Evening.

5   The reason that we took the decision to sell them was because we wanted to raise money for our partner school.

At first, we made a lot of designs. This was because we wanted one that would stand out.

Then we asked some Stage 2 learners which ones they liked, because it was important to involve the younger children too.

Finally, I made sure that we had a table by the entrance on Open Evening. This was because we wanted to have a place to be organised in and be seen.

Peer feedback (approx. 5–10 mins)

Pair each learner with a partner from a different group. Ask them to think about features of each other's reflection, how clear it is, how the ideas of others have changed the way they think about the issue, how their skills have developed.

Getting better at reflection skills: Lesson 9

In Lesson 9, learners focus on improving personal contribution, by suggesting improvements; and on teamwork, by being presented with some potential challenges and being asked to identify solutions. They also focus on personal viewpoints, by considering some potential barriers to change and identifying potential ways of removing these barriers; and on personal learning, by looking at some potential barriers to learning and suggesting potential ways of removing them.

CAMBRIDGE STAGE 6 REFLECTION LEARNING OBJECTIVES

4.1 Personal contribution: Discuss the impact of personal contribution to teamwork

4.2 Teamwork: Identify benefits and challenges of working together to achieve a shared outcome

4.3 Personal viewpoints: Discuss ways that personal ideas may have been influenced by new information or the ideas of others

4.4 Personal learning: Identify skills learnt or improved during an activity

LESSON LEARNING GOALS

To get better at:

- finding ways in which I can help my team

- understanding some of the benefits and challenges of working together as a team

- understanding how new information or the ideas of others have changed the way people think about a topic

- recognising ways to improve my personal skills.

Resources needed

Learner's Skills Book 6

Downloadable 4.14

Challenge topic (e.g. Sharing Planet Earth, Keeping healthy, Moving goods and people)

Prior learning (approx. 5–10 mins)

Good for: Activating prior knowledge.

Activity: Learners reflect on an action that they have completed as part of a team recently and are asked to identify: how working as part of a team helped them; what their team's goal was; what they did to help their team achieve its goal; what they think could have made their team work (even) better and what the challenges they found about working in a team were.

Ways of working: There needs to be time for individual reflection. Some focused pair talk time could be allocated prior to taking ideas from the class.

Differentiation: Support learners by suggesting recent examples from across the curriculum or in learners' broader local experiences. Challenge learners to deepen/justify their answers, for example if their team was a sports team and their goal was 'to win the game' does that mean that the performance was poor by definition if they failed in that objective? How could such an objective be redefined to make it more process orientated?

Suggested answers:

1. A hockey match

2. Goalkeeper

3. The defenders tackled the strikers before they could shoot.

4. To perform to the best of our ability

5. I made three saves, one from short range.

6. Moving into space sooner so that there was always someone to pass to.

7. Changing tactics when the opposing team did something different from what we'd been expecting.

Starter activity (approx. 10–15 mins)

Good for: Learners to apply their understanding of the challenges of team projects (and how to resolve them) more broadly.

Activity: Read through the learning goals for this lesson with learners at the beginning of this activity. Learners match a set of challenges to an appropriate response based on the potential solutions.

Ways of working: Learners work in pairs for discussion.

Differentiation: Support learners by encouraging them to rule out evidently inappropriate responses in the first instance. Challenge learners to develop/deepen their answers; for example, having a clear action plan that sets out the actions and who is responsible for each of them, could sort out the problem of taking responsibility appropriately. What would one look like? What headings would be good to have?

Suggested answers: See the Worked Example in Downloadable 4.14.

Main activity (approx. 20–25 mins)

Good for. Learners to reflect on the given outcomes of a team project and suggest ways of improving them.

Activity: Learners read Arun's reflection on a project he did with his team two years ago and suggest how he could have improved his group action. Afterwards, they share their ideas in the class discussion.

Ways of working: This could be done individually, in pairs or in groups with individual members taking responsibility for a specific question.

Differentiation: Support learners by discussing the limitations of the project as outlined prior to identifying possible solutions. Would any of the suggested actions from the Starter activity have helped? Which ones? How? Why? Challenge learners to deepen their answers, for example by focusing on the root cause of the limited outcomes of the project. What was actually achieved? Why was this so limited? What was insecure in the way the project was conceived?

Suggested answers: Learners might respond to Arun as follows:

Well done for tackling an issue like healthy eating.

1   I like the way you focus on an important issue. Next time, you could try conducting a survey first. This would help you to find out what people already know/think before you take a course of action.

2   To improve your teamwork, you could try clear action plan that sets out the actions and states why each of them matters to the end goal.

3   To develop the way you think about an issue, next time you could consider different perspectives. If your class already know about healthy foods, could you encourage them to share their understanding with people who don't, for example the younger children?

4   To make more of the opportunities to improve your skills, next time you could try volunteering to do something you have never tried before.

Taking it further: Lessons 7–9

The reflection on working as part of a team throughout the unit could be used as a stimulus for learners to evaluate strategies they have so far used in a given sport. Learners could be challenged to come up with a new approach which promotes greater effectiveness among team members. The use of peer coaching could be used as part of this process and new strategies for providing effective feedback introduced.

> Collaboration

SKILLS SECTION	CROSS-CURRICULAR LINKS	TOPICS MODELLED
	Learners have opportunities to apply their knowledge and understanding of, and skills in:	
Starting with	Science: thinking and working scientifically • Sort, group and classify objects, materials and living things through testing, observation and using secondary information • Use a range of secondary information sources to research and select relevant evidence to answer questions Language skills: speaking and listening • Show consideration of another point of view • Extend a discussion by building on own and other's ideas • Encourage others to take turns in a discussion	Reduce, re-use, recycle Sharing Planet Earth Improving communication
Developing	Science: thinking and working scientifically • Sort, group and classify objects, materials and living things through testing, observation and using secondary information • Use a range of secondary information sources to research and select relevant evidence to answer questions Computing: • Using flowcharts to plot solutions when solving problems Technology: • Understanding of how to strengthen, and reinforce structures Language skills: speaking and listening • Structure information to aid the listener's understanding of the main and subsidiary points	Sharing Planet Earth Using energy
Getting better at	Science: science in context • Use science to support points when discussing issues, situations or actions • Discuss how the use of science and technology can have positive and negative environmental effects on their local area PE: • evaluating performance in group work	Sharing Planet Earth Improving communication

The cross-curricular links in this table are reproduced from Cambridge International curriculum frameworks. This Cambridge International copyright material is reproduced under licence and remains the intellectual property of Cambridge Assessment International Education.

Starting with collaboration skills: Lesson 1

In Lesson 1, learners focus on starting to learn about cooperation and interdependence; and engaging in teamwork, by commenting critically on an existing plan and making revisions to it.

> **CAMBRIDGE STAGE 6 COLLABORATION LEARNING OBJECTIVES**
>
> 5.1 Cooperation and interdependence: The team plan and divide tasks fairly to achieve a shared outcome, considering skills of team members and time available
>
> 5.2 Engaging in teamwork: The team member introduces useful ideas that are likely to help achieve a shared outcome and works positively to solve problems faced by the team

> **LESSON LEARNING GOALS**
>
> To start to:
>
> • work with others to plan a task
>
> • work well with others to solve a problem.

Resources needed

Learner's Skills Book 6

Downloadables 5.1, 5.2 and 5.3

Challenge topic (e.g. Reduce, re-use, recycle, Sharing Planet Earth, Improving communication)

Prior learning (approx. 5–10 mins)

Good for: Building on previous knowledge.

Activity: Ask learners to read the brief personal reflection text given in Downloadable 5.1, and to match sections of the text to the headings provided.

Ways of working: Learners work individually on the task to begin with before getting into pairs or small groups to discuss their work. Stage a plenary session to check answers with the whole class.

Differentiation: Support learners by checking their understanding of the text by using questioning. Challenge learners to explain their answers and to

comment on the structure of the text, which shows how the writer's thinking on the topic develops and changes as a result of facts learnt about it, and how this also leads to changes in the writer's behaviour.

Suggested answers: For a Worked Example see Downloadable 5.2.

Starter activity (approx. 10–15 mins)

Good for: Starting to consider the factors that underpin effective planning in order to achieve a shared team goal.

Activity: Read through the learning goals for this lesson with learners at the beginning of this activity. Ask learners to read a short discussion by members of a team planning how to achieve a shared goal and the list of tasks that they come up with in order to achieve that goal. They then analyse the tasks in terms of the time they will need, what skills are required to achieve them and how they can be fairly allocated to members of the team.

Ways of working: Give learners in groups the opportunity to discuss their responses to the class discussion questions before staging a plenary session in which groups can report back on their thinking, and respond to each other's ideas.

Differentiation: Support learners by checking their understanding of the tasks listed in the table by using questioning. Challenge learners to analyse the tasks in terms of the time they will take, the skills required to complete them successfully and how they can be divided fairly among the members of the team.

Suggested answers: There are no definitive answers to the class discussion questions. Accept any reasonable responses, especially those supported by evidence or reasoning.

1   Encourage learners to reach the conclusion that time can be saved by allocating some tasks to individuals who will work on their own, so that work can be carried out on several tasks simultaneously. Other tasks might be more quickly completed by two or more team members working together.

2   As well as pointing out that analysis skills may help team members to understand what each task requires in terms of specific skills sets (e.g. the ability to combine images and text will be needed to create effective posters; craft skills may be needed to convert plastic bottles into pen holders,

etc.), encourage learners to think in terms of collaborative skills, such as being able to work individually on a task, while at the same time having an understanding of how it contributes to the team's shared goal. Communication skills such as being able to listen to others' contributions in group discussions will also be important.

3   Having considered the importance of factors such as time and skills with regard to successfully achieving the team's shared goal, encourage learners to think in different ways about what 'fairly' might mean when it comes to dividing tasks between the team members. Is it a matter of everyone doing the same number of tasks, or of everyone spending equal amounts of time contributing to the team effort? Is it a question of matching the most appropriate tasks to individual team members' particular skills and knowledge?

Main activity (approx. 20–25 mins)

Good for: Starting to analyse the effectiveness of planning towards achieving a shared team goal.

Activity: Ask learners to look at an example of planning designed to achieve a shared team goal and to comment on how effective it is.

Ways of working: Learners work in groups to discuss

the example of a plan and to come up with suggestions for improving it. Hand out Downloadable 5.3 for them to work on. Give the groups the opportunity to discuss the changes to the plan that they would like to propose before staging a plenary session in which the groups report back to the class and respond to others' ideas.

Differentiation: Support learners by checking their understanding of the plan by using questioning. Challenge learners to come up with alternative ways of achieving the team's shared goal to that shown in the example.

Suggested answers: There are no definitive answers. Accept any reasonable responses, especially those supported by evidence or reasoning. Encourage learners to point out some of the shortcomings in the plan. For example, Marcus appears to be doing less than the others, and the amount of time each team member is given to complete their tasks is unequal. Are there times when one or more team members will be waiting for others to complete their tasks before they can start working on a new task? Is it really necessary for all four team members to make stickers? If only Zara and Arun worked on making the questionnaire, Sofia and Marcus could spend more time on making stickers, and so on.

Challenge learners to come up with a different planning format if they feel this example isn't the most effective way of presenting the information.

Starting with collaboration skills: Lesson 2

In Lesson 2, learners focus on starting to learn about cooperation and interdependence; and on engaging in teamwork, by asking learners to create a group plan that aims at achieving a shared goal.

CAMBRIDGE STAGE 6 COLLABORATION LEARNING OBJECTIVES

5.1 Cooperation and interdependence: The team plan and divide tasks fairly to achieve a shared outcome, considering skills of team members and time available

5.2 Engaging in teamwork: The team member introduces useful ideas that are likely to help achieve a shared outcome and works positively to solve problems faced by the team

LESSON LEARNING GOALS

To start to:
* work with others to plan a task
* work well with others to solve a problem.

Resources needed

Learner's Skills Book 6

Challenge topic (e.g. Reduce, re-use, recycle, Sharing Planet Earth, Improving communication)

Prior learning (approx. 5–10 mins)

Good for: Building on previous knowledge.

Activity: Ask learners to read a short text about how a group solved a problem that arose while they were planning for teamwork and to match the collaboration skills to the names in the text.

Ways of working: Learners work individually on the task to begin with before getting into pairs or small groups to discuss their work. Stage a plenary session to check answers with the whole class.

Differentiation: Support learners by checking their understanding of the text by using questioning. Challenge learners to identify the collaboration skills demonstrated by different members of the team.

Suggested answers: 1: Zara, Sofia; 2: Marcus, Arun; 3: Sofia; 4: Zara

Starter activity (approx. 10–15 mins)

Good for: Starting to plan how to work as a team towards achieving a shared goal.

Activity: Read through the learning goals for this lesson with learners at the beginning of this activity. Ask learners in groups to choose an issue to focus on and to plan how to work towards a shared goal. Encourage learners to choose an issue of local relevance but, if possible, to avoid plastic pollution, which is the topic focus of the previous lesson.

Ways of working: Learners work in groups, ideally of four. Within each group, roles can be assigned to facilitate planning.

Differentiation: Support learners by allocating clearly defined roles within the group (e.g. facilitator, recorder, timekeeper, reporter, etc.). Challenge learners to define and allocate their own roles.

Suggested answers: There are no definitive answers, as the tasks listed by each group may vary according to the issue they have chosen, or their own ideas about what would make an effective stall. The number of tasks envisaged as being necessary may also vary from group to group. (The plan from the previous lesson can serve as a model. Alternatively, learners may prefer to work with a different planning format – see Downloadable 5.3 from Lesson 1 as an example.)

Main activity (approx. 20–25 mins)

Good for: Starting to divide tasks fairly between members of a team and resolving any problems that may arise.

Activity: Ask learners to complete a plan showing how the tasks they have listed in the previous activity can be fairly divided between members of the team, how long each should take, and the sequence in which the tasks will be completed.

Ways of working: Learners continue to work in the same groups.

Differentiation: Support learners by reminding them of the collaboration skills that they may find useful for this activity (see the Prior learning activity). Challenge learners to resolve any problems that arise between members of the team so that the planning can be completed successfully.

Suggested answers: Plans will vary from group to group. For the class discussion questions:

1   Encourage groups to report on how successfully they defined roles in the group to facilitate the planning process.

2   Encourage groups to report back on how well they feel they have achieved the goal of dividing tasks fairly between the different members and on how successful they have been in timing and sequencing the work of the team. Another issue to explore here is how well the skills and knowledge of the different members of the team have been matched to the tasks they have each been allocated.

3   Encourage learners to discuss how they resolved any conflicts or other difficulties that arose during the planning process. Where there were disagreements between different members of the team over how to proceed, what solutions were applied? (These could include: compromise solutions proposed by themselves or other members of the team, where concessions are made by both sides; voting by team members to find a solution that a majority are in favour of; making the decision of the group leader final, both sides having had the opportunity to present arguments in favour of doing things their way, etc.).

For an example of a completed plan, look back to Lesson 1 in the Learner's Skills Book.

Peer feedback (approx. 5–10 mins)

Pair learners, preferably with a partner from a different group. Ask learners to report to their partner on aspects of the teamwork activity they have just taken part in using the prompts. Their partner then feeds back to them on two positive aspects of their collaboration, and one area for improvement, which they record in their Learner's Skills Book.

Taking it further: Lessons 1–2

If possible, allow learners in their groups to execute their plan from Lesson 2 by giving them the opportunity to create a stall that promotes awareness of an issue they have chosen. Having done this, they could then evaluate how effective their plan was in practice. Did they divide up the work fairly among themselves? Did they allow enough time for each task they planned? Did they plan to do things in the correct sequence?

Developing collaboration skills: Lesson 3

In Lesson 3, learners focus on developing their cooperation and interdependence by planning a task to achieve a shared outcome. They reflect on their prior experience of working with others to achieve a goal. They consider a range of appropriate actions to address given problems or to meet identified goals, then decide on an issue to focus on and begin to consider what actions it might be appropriate to undertake.

CAMBRIDGE STAGE 6 COLLABORATION LEARNING OBJECTIVES

5.1 Cooperation and interdependence: The team plan and divide tasks fairly to achieve a shared outcome, considering skills of team members and time available

LESSON LEARNING GOALS

To develop my knowledge and understanding about:

- how to start to plan a task to achieve a shared outcome.

Resources needed

Learner's Skills Book 6

Downloadable 5.4

Challenge topic (e.g. Sharing Planet Earth, Using energy)

Previous examples of working in a team

Prior to the lesson, have a discussion auditing global issues: what they are, how they impact on the school / local area and what is being done

Prior learning (approx. 5–10 mins)

Good for: Activating prior experience and understanding of collaboration.

Activity: Learners are provided with a scaffold in the Learner's Skills Book. They use it to identify similar experiences they have had. They consider the processes that led to an outcome and their feelings on having accomplished the task.

Ways of working: Learners reflect individually on the questions before pair and whole class discussion.

Differentiation: Support learners by providing examples from their recent experience. It may be appropriate to seek examples from the previous class teacher. Challenge learners to identify any obstacles they confronted and how these were successfully overcome.

Suggested answers: There are no definitive answers. Accept any reasonable responses, from learners' past experiences, for example:

- I was the costume monitor in the class production. I made sure everyone had their costume ready at the right time – and it was put away ready for the next show.

- I was the art monitor in Class 4. I made sure all the brushes and paints were ready at the start of the lesson – and the trays were clean at the end.

- My brother had been an art monitor last year. He gave me some good tips. With help, we can now get the equipment all sorted out in two minutes and thirty seconds.

Starter activity (approx. 10–15 mins)

Good for: Learners to develop their understanding of action planning.

Activity: Read through the learning goals for this lesson with learners at the beginning of this activity. Learners are given different elements of a flowchart leading from problem to solution. They have to complete it. The amount of scaffolding is progressively reduced.

Ways of working: Learners to work in pairs to discuss answers.

Differentiation: Support learners by helping them understand that the outcome is the opposite of the problem – that is, a solution. The action is something that will bring the outcome about. If necessary, model another example for them. Challenge learners to consider a range of possible actions and consider which would be the most appropriate/efficient/effective. Challenge them further to justify their response.

Suggested answers: See the Worked Example in Downloadable 5.4.

Main activity (approx. 20–25 mins)

Good for: Learners to apply their understanding of planning a task to their own issue.

Activity: Learners identify shared problems, suggest actions (working together) and identify shared outcomes.

Ways of working: You may wish to specify a local issue based on an audit of needs. Alternatively, you may wish to give your learners a wider choice. This is likely to depend on their prior experience of taking responsibility / problem solving. Learners should be grouped in teams that will last through the process beyond this lesson to taking and evaluating an action. Pairs could come up with an action each prior to sharing their ideas. A group of six would therefore have three ideas to evaluate.

Differentiation: Support learners by discussing the starter examples with them. Explore how this process can be applied to their context. Challenge learners to consider how different actions may have different impacts on different groups of people, for example younger children. How does this influence their decision regarding whether an action is appropriate?

Suggested answers: See the Worked Example for the flowchart in Downloadable 5.6. For the follow-on questions, responses on the topic of plastic pollution might be:

- The task that we are prioritising at this stage is setting up a 'No Plastic club'.
- This is because, firstly, plastic pollution is a major global problem.
- In addition, we know not enough is being done in our area – the local stream is full of it.
- Furthermore, we have some confident people in our group. They won't feel shy talking to others.
- Finally, we already have ideas for a 'No Plastic club' badge.

For the class discussion, support learners by helping them to ask questions of their peers to clarify their plans before they evaluate. Challenge learners to evaluate the impacts of the proposed action from different perspectives. Responses based on the 'No Plastic club' might be:

1   There is clearly an issue with plastic in the area if the stream is full of it. The nature and extent of the problem could be clarified further.

2   The 'No Plastic club' idea would encourage a sense of being part of a shared goal. Greater clarity on what behaviours need to be changed would help here. Are children responsible for the problem? Or are they part of the solution by raising awareness to others?

3   The objective 'school grounds and the area outside the school [being] clear of litter' has some clarity if they are able to define what they mean by area outside the school. A 'plastic count' in defined areas at specific times could indeed quantify success.

4   'Children first learn about plastic pollution then organise action squads' suggests a number of possible team actions. What these tasks might be and how they might divide these tasks up lacks clarity at present.

5   The clearing up needs some risk assessment. Site staff should have access to relevant guidelines and, potentially, equipment. It would need a level of supervision and guidance – especially for the area outside school. Nevertheless, there is a lot that a group of children could achieve given resourcefulness and resilience.

Developing collaboration skills: Lesson 4

In Lesson 4, learners focus on developing their skills in engaging in teamwork and making suggestions, by considering ways that their team would solve a given challenge and then evaluating how well their team worked together.

CAMBRIDGE STAGE 6 COLLABORATION LEARNING OBJECTIVES

5.2 Engaging in teamwork: The team member introduces useful ideas that are likely to help achieve a shared outcome and works positively to solve problems faced by the team

LESSON LEARNING GOALS

To develop my knowledge and understanding about:

- introducing useful ideas that help to achieve a shared outcome

- working positively to solve a problem faced by the team.

Resources needed

Learner's Skills Book 6

Downloadable 5.5

Challenge topic (e.g. Sharing Planet Earth, Using energy)

A quantity of recycled paper

10 cm of tape per group

Some small weights of 100 g

Relevant images of towers and constructions for challenge

Risk assessment: Ensure the groups do not suspend weights too high so that they could cause an injury if they fall. If learners are challenged to make a tall construction, ensure they are not climbing on furniture. Ensure relevant school policies are consulted and adhered to.

Prior learning (approx. 5–10 mins)

Good for: Learners to activate their prior understanding of how to plan a task for a group. NB it is likely that their ideas will be subject to compromise – this is part of the process.

Activity: Tell your learners that their challenge is to make a tower out of recycled paper that will support a weight of 100 g for 30 seconds. Tell them that each team will have just 10 cm of tape to use. You may wish to specify additional constraints on the project, for example the amount of paper available. Learners plan out how they envisage their group could make a tower out of recycled paper that will support a weight of 100 g for 30 seconds. You may wish to write the challenge on the board.

Ways of working: This activity needs to be conducted individually so learners can evaluate how effectively they plan was for the whole group's work.

Differentiation: Support learners by providing images, for example of bridge constructions. Challenge learners to justify their chosen method.

Suggested answers: Learners' answers will vary depend on their prior experience of teamwork. Look for useful ideas that help to achieve the shared outcome. Look for an appropriate sequence.

Starter activity (approx. 10–15 mins)

Good for: A practical experience of teamwork that can be evaluated.

Activity: Read through the learning goals for this lesson with learners at the beginning of this activity. Remind your learners that their challenge is to make a tower out of recycled paper that will support a weight of 100 g for 30 seconds and that each team will have just 10 cm of tape to use. Remind them also of any additional constraints that you specified at the beginning.

Ways of working: There are a number of different ways in which this activity can be approached. One way is to specify that it should be conducted without talking. Limited quantities of newspaper could be used as this is challenging to make robust structures from. Learners then evaluate the process.

Differentiation: Support learners by providing some appropriate images of robust structures (e.g. suspension bridges) at the start. Alternatively, challenge learners by, for example, not giving initial ideas; providing limited quantities of materials; providing additional weight to support. The level of challenge you provide will be based on your prior assessment of your learners' technology skills.

Suggested answers:

1   At first, I thought that *tubes* would be a good idea.

2   I later found out that *they collapsed easily*.

3   A positive contribution I made to the group was *pointing to the chair for an idea*.

4   One good thing about working in a group was that *you have more hands to hold the structure*.

5   One challenge of working in a group was *we didn't have the same idea – this made it harder to agree*.

6   One way I could have improved my contribution to the group would have been to *look at robust shapes, for example triangles*.

7   If I were to do the activity again, I would *save some tape until the end*.

Main activity (approx. 20–25 mins)

Good for: Breaking down the process of developing an action to meet a specified objective.

Activity: Groups develop actions based on the stimulus questions: What? When? Where? Who? Why? Learners either develop a series of actions that could help Arun and Zara meet their goal of encouraging children to switch off lights. Or they develop actions that could help their group meet their own goal.

Ways of working: Learners work in groups for this activity.

Differentiation: Support learners by working step-by-step through an additional example or more

until the process becomes clear. Challenge learners to justify their proposed course of action. Is it appropriate? Would it be an efficient use of time/labour/resources? How likely would it be to meet the goal set?

Suggested answers: See the Worked Example in Downloadable 5.5.

Peer feedback (approx. 5 mins)

Pair each learner with a partner. Ask them to find out to what extent from their partner's perspective they worked well as part of a team. Support learners by providing positive examples of collaboration you observed. Challenge learners to develop reasoned explanations of how/when collaborative skills led to improved outcomes. Ask them to provide specific examples.

Taking it further: Lessons 3–4

Arun and Zara came up with ideas for ways to encourage children to turn off lights. Learners could be given the challenge of developing ideas to encourage their peers to save energy (or to encourage positive action with regard to an issue that you are working on) in different ways. This would involve learners presenting work in a visually appealing way. Techniques such as trimming, mounting, titles, labels and neat gluing could be developed alongside understanding importance of planning lettering and use of space. This would provide opportunities to teach the importance of good layout in different design elements.

Getting better at collaboration skills: Lesson 5

In Lesson 5, learners focus on getting better at cooperation, interdependence and engaging in teamwork. They evaluate their previous contributions to teamwork, then use the results of this evaluation to devise an action plan, implement it and reflect on how their relevant skills have developed.

LESSON LEARNING GOALS

To get better at:

- working with others to plan a task, deciding how long it will take to complete
- working independently on tasks that help to achieve a team goal.

Resources needed

Learner's Skills Book 6

Downloadable 5.6

Challenge topic (e.g. Sharing Planet Earth, Improving communication)

Prior learning (approx. 5–10 mins)

Good for: Learners to activate their prior understanding of what characterises effective teams and what characterises effective individual team players.

Activity: Based on their experiences of teamwork (including in the previous lesson), learners answer four questions on teamwork.

Ways of working: This activity may provoke interesting discussion if learners are given time to develop their own individual perspectives.

Differentiation: Support learners by reminding them of what happened last time they engaged in a team activity – particularly if some time has elapsed since they last did so. Challenge learners to develop their explanation of effective teamwork by clearly identifying cause and effect.

Suggested answers:

1   A good team member always: offers helpful ideas; suggests practical solutions; listens to others' suggestions; has a positive approach to working with others, sees tasks through to successful conclusions; is sensitive to others' perspectives and proactive in resolving any conflicts within the team; respects others' efforts and encourages other team members to participate positively.

2   A good team always: has a positive approach to communicating from start to finish and is proactive in resolving any conflicts; appreciates that from time to time different perspectives make these inevitable; makes sure that the division of tasks between members is efficient and at the same time allows team members to develop their skills; works together until a shared goal is reached.

3   A good team member never: rejects helpful ideas; refuses to implement practical solutions; ignores others' suggestions when they are offered positively; has a negative approach to working with others; drops tasks before they have reached successful conclusions; ignores others' perspectives or intentionally worsens any conflicts within the team; is disrespectful towards others' efforts or discourages other team members from participate positively.

4   A good team never: isolates team members from the process or allows conflicts to simmer; rejects perspectives just because they differ; tolerates inefficient working that does not allows team members to make a positive contribution; lacks understanding of what the shared goal is or gives up before it is reached.

Starter activity (approx. 10–15 mins)

Good for: Learners to apply their understanding of what makes effective teams and effective members within them to evaluate their own approach and develop ways they can improve.

Activity: Read through the learning goals for this lesson with learners at the beginning of this activity. Based on their experiences (including in the previous lesson), learners are given the opportunity to evaluate their own approach to teamwork by identifying a response that best matches their individual approach. They use these to develop two aspects they can improve on – as individuals and as teams.

Ways of working: This will need to be approached with sensitivity as learners' negative experiences of teamwork can impact negatively on self-esteem. The activity should be introduced as an opportunity to reflect on past experiences of teamwork proactively – with previous setbacks seen as an opportunity to learn from them and put in place strategies to overcome them in future.

Differentiation: It is often the case that self-assessment can be harsh, so support learners by questioning that helps them to identify step-by-step factually what happened last time they engaged in a team activity. Challenge learners to develop their explanation of how to improve by being specific about likely consequences, for example 'If, . . . then the result will be . . . because . . . An example of this would be . . . '

Suggested answers: Learners should give their own responses to the tick-box options. Responses to the follow-on questions might be:

1   To be an even better team member, next time I will aim to listen more carefully to others' ideas.

2   This is because teams that have different ideas to draw on are more likely to find solutions.

3   To be an even better team, next time we must aim to make sure our members can develop their skills.

4   This is because, if someone in the group is really good at something, they can help the others by teaching them.

Main activity (flexible timing)

Good for: Learners to break down an overall task into specific actions for each team member and monitor its progress.

Activity: Learners complete an action plan that asks them to identify specific actions, responsible team members, deadlines, resources needed and progress.

Ways of working: This could be applied to a short-term task – for example 'tidy the classroom' – in the first instance. When they are familiar with the format, learners apply their understanding of the process to longer-term projects such as 'improve the proportion of journeys taken to our school using sustainable transport'.

Differentiation: Support learners by encouraging them to first break down the overall objective into a sequence of discrete steps. Challenge learners to develop specific, measurable, achievable realistic and time limited targets.

Suggested answers: See Downloadable 5.6 for Worked Examples of a short-term and longer-term action plan.

Taking it further: Lesson 5

Encourage learners to reflect on their experiences of working as a team and to draw up a balanced list of benefits and challenges of teamwork. As a class, identify which aspects of teamwork are generally considered to be the most challenging. Ask learners to work in groups and assign a different challenge of teamwork to each group. Ask the groups to come up with solutions for overcoming their challenge. Encourage groups to create slogans that will help motivate learners to overcome the challenges and display these around the classroom.

> Communication

SKILLS SECTION	CROSS-CURRICULAR LINKS *Learners have opportunities to apply their knowledge and understanding of, and skills in:*	TOPICS MODELLED
Starting with	Science: science in context • Use science to support points when discussing issues, situations or actions • Discuss how the use of science and technology can have positive and negative environmental effects on their local area Language skills: reading • Recognise explicit and implicit ways in which the theme of a text is conveyed • Explore and recognise the key features of text structure in a range of different texts	Sharing Planet Earth
Developing	Language skills: writing • Use organisational features appropriate to the text type, e.g. bulleted and numbered lists • Manage the development of an idea across an extended piece of writing, e.g. by linking the end to the beginning • Develop writing for a purpose using language and features appropriate for a range of text types	Moving goods and people
Getting better at	Language skills: speaking and listening • Plan and deliver independent and group presentations confidently to a range of audiences, adapting presentations appropriately to the audience Language skills: writing • Evaluate own and others' writing, suggesting improvements for sense, accuracy and content, including to enhance the effect Geography: human geography • understanding human activities and the consequences of change on the environment	Moving goods and people

The cross-curricular links in this table are reproduced from Cambridge International curriculum frameworks. This Cambridge International copyright material is reproduced under licence and remains the intellectual property of Cambridge Assessment International Education.

Starting with communication skills: Lesson 1

In Lesson 1, learners focus on starting to communicate information, by presenting information on a topic, and on listening and responding, by listening to the information presented by others and responding with questions when appropriate.

CAMBRIDGE STAGE 6 COMMUNICATION LEARNING OBJECTIVES

6.1 Communicating information: Present information clearly with an appropriate structure and with some reference to sources where appropriate

6.2 Listening and responding: Listen to ideas and information about an issue and ask questions relevant to the issue

LESSON LEARNING GOALS

To start to:

- tell other people about a topic so that they can understand it better

- listen to what someone tells me about a topic and respond by asking questions.

Resources needed

Learner's Skills Book 6

Downloadables 6.1, 6.2 and 6.3

Challenge topic (e.g. Sharing Planet Earth)

Prior learning (approx. 5–10 mins)

Good for: Building on previous knowledge.

Activity: Ask learners to read a short text and identify some of its features relating to the process of collaboration.

Ways of working: Learners work individually on the task to begin with, before getting into pairs or small groups to discuss their work. Stage a plenary session to check answers with the whole class.

Differentiation: Support learners by checking their understanding of the text by using questioning. Challenge learners to explain their answers with reference to the text.

Suggested answers: a = 4; b = 1; c = 5; d= 4, e = 2. See Downloadable 6.1 for a Worked Example.

Starter activity (approx. 10–15 mins)

Good for: Starting to listen to what others say about a topic, responding with questions where necessary.

Activity: Read through the learning goals for this lesson with learners at the beginning of this activity. Ask learners to read the short text in the Learner's Skills Book that provides the context for this and the Main activity and then to discuss attitudes towards zoos.

Ways of working: Give learners the opportunity to talk about the topic in pairs or small groups before staging a class discussion. Encourage learners to express their views on the topic and to respond to others by asking questions.

Differentiation: Support learners by checking their understanding of key vocabulary for this topic, for example extinct, rare, endangered, captivity, and so on. Challenge learners to come up with arguments for and against zoos.

Suggested answers: Accept any reasonable answers, especially those supported by evidence or reasoning, or based on the learners' first-hand experience of visiting zoos.

Main activity (approx. 20–25 mins)

Good for: Starting to tell others about a topic, and starting to listen to others talking about a topic, asking questions for clarification where necessary.

Activity: Give each learner in a group a different source (see Downloadable 6.2) and ask them to tell each other about the arguments for and against zoos found in the source. Learners should be encouraged to do this orally.

Ways of working: Ask learners to work in groups, ideally with four learners in each group. Stage a plenary at the end of the activity in which learners can respond to the arguments they have encountered in the sources. Encourage groups to reach a consensus on whether or not they are in favour of supporting zoos.

Differentiation: Support learners by checking their understanding of the information in their source by using questioning. Challenge learners to identify which arguments are for zoos and which are against. Encourage them to find connections between different pieces of information in different sources. Challenge learners further to come up with additional arguments for or against zoos.

Suggested answers: See the Worked Example in Downloadable 6.3. Responses to the class discussion questions might be:

1   Accept any of the arguments in favour of zoos, providing it is supported by evidence and/or reasoning. For example, zoos prevent rare animals becoming extinct – this is important because once an animal is extinct, it is lost for ever.

2   Accept any of the arguments against zoos, providing it is supported by evidence and/or reasoning. For example, zoos can never exactly re-create an animal's natural habitat, so it would be better to protect habitats where all the animals' needs can be met.

Starting with communication skills: Lesson 2

In Lesson 2, learners focus on starting to communicate information, by planning and delivering a presentation that argues for a particular point of view; and on listening and responding, by listening to presentations delivered by others, and responding by asking questions where appropriate.

CAMBRIDGE STAGE 6 COMMUNICATION LEARNING OBJECTIVES

6.1   Communicating information: Present information clearly with an appropriate structure and with some reference to sources where appropriate

6.2   Listening and responding: Listen to ideas and information about an issue and ask questions relevant to the issue

LESSON LEARNING GOALS

To start to:

- tell other people about a topic so that they can understand it better
- listen to what someone tells me about a topic and respond by asking questions.

Resources needed

Learner's Skills Book 6

Downloadables 6.3, 6.4, 6.5 and 6.6

Challenge topic (e.g. Sharing Planet Earth)

Prior learning (approx. 5–10 mins)

Good for: Building on previous knowledge.

Activity: Ask learners to read a short argument text and to analyse the arguments it presents.

Ways of working: Learners work individually to begin with before getting into pairs or small groups to discuss their work. Stage a plenary session to check answers with the whole class.

Differentiation: Support learners by checking their understanding of the text by using questioning. Challenge learners to explain their answers with reference to the text, and to come up with more arguments relating to the topic.

Suggested answers: See the Worked Example in Downloadable 6.4.

Starter activity (approx. 10–15 mins)

Good for: Starting to think about how to present an argument for or against a topic.

Activity: Read through the learning goals for this lesson with learners at the beginning of this activity. Ask learners to review the arguments for and against zoos from the previous lesson and to decide as a group which side to support. Learners then identify three arguments to support their case.

Ways of working: Learners work in groups (ideally the same groups as in the previous lesson), reaching a group consensus on whether or not to support zoos and on which arguments to use.

Differentiation: Support learners by establishing clear roles within the groups, so that decisions can be reached by consensus. Challenge learners to think about how to organise and present an argument.

Suggested answers: Allow learners time to arrive at a group decision. Accept any three arguments from the previous lesson (see Downloadable 6.3) provided that they are consistent with the stance (for or against) adopted by the group.

For the class discussion questions:

1 Encourage learners to think about how to introduce their argument by defining the topic clearly and stating their point of view (for or against); to present a sequence of clearly stated arguments in support of that position; to support each argument by developing the idea in more detail and/or by offering specific examples; and to reach a clear conclusion, restating their point of view.

2 Encourage learners to think about using rhetorical devices such as addressing the audience directly (You . . .), using expressive gestures, eye contact and tone of voice, and so on.

Main activity (approx. 20–25 mins)

Good for: Starting to plan a presentation to be given in front of an audience that will inform them about a topic with a view to persuading them to agree with a particular point of view.

Activity: Ask learners to plan a group presentation arguing for or against zoos, using the template in Downloadable 6.5.

Ways of working: Learners work in the same groups as for the Starter activity to plan their presentation. They then receive peer feedback on their planned presentation, modifying it accordingly. Groups should then be given the chance to present their argument to the class. This can be the responsibility of one group member (i.e. the reporter), or the responsibility can be shared by the whole group, each member delivering a different part of the presentation. Allow time for others

to ask questions and respond after each presentation.

Differentiation: Support learners by establishing clear roles within the group, so that decisions can be reached by consensus. Challenge learners to refine their arguments by adding more specific detail and/ or examples.

Suggested answers: For a Worked Example, of the arguments for and against zoos, see Downloadable 6.6.

Peer feedback (approx. 5–10 mins)

Pair each learner with a partner from a different group. Where any of the answers to the questions about their plan is 'NO', encourage learners to come up with changes to the plan, perhaps through discussion with their partner.

Taking it further: Lessons 1–2

Encourage learners to investigate an issue of their own choosing which they are either strongly for or strongly against. They should assemble arguments to support their viewpoint. Organise a debate about the issue, with speakers for or against presenting their arguments in front of the class. Encourage listeners to respond by asking questions. Alternatively, continue to focus on the issue of zoos by investigating zoos in the local area. If possible, invite a speaker from a local zoo to visit the class to explain what the zoo does, and to face questions from the learners. Explore ways in which the learners could support the work of the zoo or of a local wildlife conservation organisation, possibly through fund-raising activities or an awareness-raising campaign.

Developing communication skills: Lesson 3

In Lesson 3, learners focus on developing their skills in presenting information clearly. They are given a model with an appropriate structure and with some appropriate reference to sources. They then use this model to plan a persuasive discussion on their own chosen topic.

CAMBRIDGE STAGE 6 COMMUNICATION LEARNING OBJECTIVES

6.1 Communicating information: Present information clearly with an appropriate structure and with some reference to sources where appropriate

LESSON LEARNING GOALS

To develop my knowledge and understanding about:

- how to present information on a topic using a clear structure

- how to refer to sources that I have used.

Resources needed

Learner's Skills Book 6

Downloadables 6.7, 6.8, 6.9, and 6.10

Challenge topic (e.g. Moving goods and people)

Prior learning (approx. 5–10 mins)

Good for: Quickfire building on previous knowledge.

Activity: Learners choose either 'zoos' or 'cycling in cities' and indicate whether they are strongly in favour, strongly against or some point in between. They then give reasons for their answer.

Ways of working: This introduction could be conducted individually. Alternatively you could specify a topic, invite the class to stand in a continuum with one side of the room 'strongly in favour' and the other 'strongly against'. Learners could then have the opportunity of sharing ideas with those whose ideas are similar prior to providing their justification.

Differentiation: Support learners by encouraging them to select relevant facts from the previous lessons. Challenge learners to develop their justification using a 'point–example–explanation' structure.

Suggested answers: Learner' answers will vary depending on which topic they choose, and their personal opinion, for example:

1   I am *strongly opposed* to *zoos.*

2   This is mainly because *I believe they deprive animas of freedom.*

3   In addition, *they cannot re-create the animals' natural habitat.*

4   Furthermore, *they forget how to hunt.*

5   Finally, *we should not look at animals as if they were objects.*

Starter activity (approx. 10–15 mins)

Good for: Showing learners how they can use both sides of an argument to make their case more persuasive.

Activity: Read through the learning goals for this lesson with learners at the beginning of this activity. Learners highlight the text provided in Downloadable 6.7 – identifying words/phrases that they could use in their own piece. This technique is sometimes referred to as 'magpieing'.

Ways of working: This could be completed individually or in supportive pairs.

Differentiation: Support learners by working through the first paragraph together. Keep working with those for whom appropriate words/phrases to select are not immediately apparent. Challenge learners to use the words/phrases for discussion of a different issue.

Suggested answers: See Downloadable 6.8.

Main activity (approx. 20–25 mins)

Good for: Learners to apply their understanding of how to present information on an issue using a modelled planning structure.

Activity: Learners plan a discussion on an issue of their choice using the framework provided in the Learner's Skills Book.

Ways of working: Learners could plan a discussion:

- on an issue of their choice

- on an global issue with local relevance that you specify

- on the issue of zoos.

Distribute copies of Arun's plan (Downloadable 6.9) to introduce the planning approach. Learners then use the skeleton plan in the Learner's Skills Book to develop their own plan.

Differentiation: Support learners by modelling the first paragraph if necessary, work together with them on the second, moving them to independence on the third. Challenge learners to develop a point, example, explanation structure. This could be planned by adding additional 'twigs' to the 'branches'.

Suggested answers: For a Worked Example on a different topic, see Downloadable 6.10.

For the class discussion, the different groups of people who might have different perspectives depends on the nature of issue – as will the people your learners are trying to influence. Central arguments may remain constant but how they presented is indeed likely to change depending on who you are talking to.

Example from the sustainable transport topic:

Who are you trying to influence?

- Parents (to encourage them to consider alternatives to driving).
- Children (to encourage them to walk or cycle if possible).

Will you have to change the arguments that you present depending on who you are talking to?

- Both groups need to know the benefits in terms of sustainability.
- Children might be more influenced by arguments that it is more enjoyable to get out of the car.

- Parents might be more influenced by arguments that it is more economical to get out of the car.

Example from the sustainable food topic:

Who are you trying to influence?

- Parents (to persuade them that school-grown vegetables are good value for money).
- Children (to encourage them to eat local vegetables).

Will you have to change the arguments that you present depending on who you are talking to?

- Both groups need to know the benefits in terms of sustainability.
- Children might be more influenced by arguments that it is more enjoyable to be involved in food production.
- Parents might be more influenced by arguments that local vegetables are just as nutritious if not more so.

Developing communication skills: Lesson 4

In Lesson 4, learners focus on developing their skills in communicating information, and in listening and responding. They use the framework created in Lesson 3 to tell their partner about their argument.

CAMBRIDGE STAGE 6 COMMUNICATION LEARNING OBJECTIVES

6.1 Communicating information: Present information clearly with an appropriate structure and with some reference to sources where appropriate

6.2 Listening and responding: Listen to ideas and information about an issue and ask questions relevant to the issue

LESSON LEARNING GOALS

To develop my knowledge and understanding about:

- how to tell other people about an issue so that they can understand it better
- how to listen to what someone tells me about an issue.

Resources needed

Learner's Skills Book 6

Downloadables 6.8, 6.9 and 6.10

Challenge topic (e.g. Moving goods and people)

Learners' completed plans from Lesson 3

Prior learning (approx. 5–10 mins)

Good for: Challenging learners to listen accurately to other people's ideas and information and summarise it.

Activity: Learners work in pairs. Each learner uses their skeleton plan to outline their discussion to their partner who in turn records key points on their own blank skeleton framework.

Ways of working: It is important for learners to sense the 'against the clock' nature of the exercise. One minute could be allocated for learners to remind themselves of what was planned in the previous lesson. Each partner could then be allocated 90 seconds speaking time. Learners should be given the opportunity to briefly compare their recording of the key points made with their partner's original plan. Who managed to record a reasonably accurate summary plan? How was this achieved?

Differentiation: Support learners by encouraging them to manage the time they have. It is better to have a single key point made from each paragraph than run out of time. Challenge learners to develop their argument using a 'point example explanation' structure. Challenge them to ensure their action points are given sufficient emphasis.

Suggested answers: See 'Arun's skeleton plan' from Lesson 3 (Downloadable 6.9) and the alternative Worked Example in Downloadable 6.10.

For the class discussion, acknowledge learners' comments about presentation skills (e.g. clear diction and eye contact are not irrelevant here) – but try to steer discussion toward how the argument is put together. Clear structures like 'identify the problem; analyse the problem; solve the problem' help.

Starter activity (approx. 10 mins)

Good for: Beginning an argument using a modelled structure.

Activity: Read through the learning goals for this lesson with learners at the beginning of this activity. Learners use the highlighted text from the introduction paragraph of Downloadable 6.8 – using appropriate words/phrases for their own piece. They use their skeleton plan from Lesson 3 for the content.

Ways of working: This is an individual activity. Point out to learners that towards the end of the lesson their partner will be giving them feedback and draw their attention to the questions in the peer feedback feature.

Differentiation: Support learners by supportive questioning. Read out the model text where words are generically relevant (similar to the highlighted text below). Verbalise 'mmm' or similar when content is specific (similar to the non-highlighted text below). Ask learners to look at their skeleton plan and say what will fit in the gap you have identified by 'mmm.' Challenge learners to provide additional phrases to those in the modelled text that would serve to emphasise the importance of the issue.

Suggested answers: Arun's structure could be applied to an introduction paragraph for a challenge topic on biodiversity as follows:

Since the millennium, there has been growing awareness of alternative ways of protecting native species. It is estimated that at least one-quarter of all native species in our country now live in urban areas, but very few city residents understand how best to care for them.

Main activity (approx. 25 mins)

Good for: Developing and concluding an argument using a modelled structure.

Activity: Learners use the highlighted text from the next three paragraphs of the previous lesson's model text – using appropriate words/phrases for their own piece. They use their skeleton plan from the previous lesson for the content.

Ways of working: See Starter activity.

Differentiation: See Starter activity.

Suggested answers:

Applying Arun's structure to the next three paragraphs of a challenge topic on energy:

The positive benefits of saving energy are well-known and children who develop good habits while they are at school are far less likely to waste energy at home. Furthermore, these children are not only reducing their own carbon footprint, but are also making a significant contribution to raising awareness in the adult population.

Many parents that we spoke to in our survey like the reassurance of knowing their child is cool and comfortable at school. They cite the potential risks faced by some children who suffer with the heat, or the dangers caused by dehydration.

However, campaigners such as Eco Energy Campaign point out that warm weather does not in itself make a school more vulnerable to high bills. Air conditioning is not the only solution.

Applying Arun's structure to a conclusion on the issue of water, food and farming:

Many scientists, such as Professor A C Mentchov, fear that food miles contribute significantly to climate change and that the planet could suffer long-term supply problems. It is therefore of the utmost importance that we work with all who can make a difference so that all of us while we are school:

*   know about and take responsibility for eating the wide range of affordable and locally produced food
*   take responsibility for growing as much as we can in the school garden
*   try to grow what we can at home
*   know about the benefits that eating fresh local fruit and vegetables brings

- push the local community for better links with local growers to be established so that all children can learn the skills they need

- join in on our weed clearing – Wednesday after school.

Peer feedback (approx. 10 mins)

Pair each learner with a partner from a different group. Remind them of the criteria they are using to give feedback. There may well be many aspects of their partner's work that could be commented on – encourage them to stick to the questions to frame their feedback.

Taking it further: Lessons 3–4

Learners could be given opportunities to plan, draft and rewrite (following on from feedback) persuasive texts advocating (or opposing) a particular solution to a local, national or global issue. Tasks of this nature provide opportunities for learners to link together paragraphs to develop their point or to influence the reader through techniques such as contrasts or unexpected shifts.

Getting better at communication skills: Lesson 5

In Lesson 5, learners focus on getting better at listening to ideas and information about an issue and asking relevant questions. Following a model, they take turns to present information and ask questions.

CAMBRIDGE STAGE 6 COMMUNICATION LEARNING OBJECTIVES

6.2 Listening and responding: Listen to ideas and information about an issue and ask questions relevant to the issue

LESSON LEARNING GOALS

To get better at:

- listening to ideas and information about an issue

- responding to what others say in class discussions by asking relevant questions.

Resources needed

Learner's Skills Book 6

Downloadable 6.11

Challenge topic (e.g. Moving goods and people)

Prior learning (approx. 5–10 mins)

Good for: Predictive assessment of learners' questioning skills.

Activity: Learners are asked to imagine that someone told them that they had a low-cost and easy-to-implement solution to the local issue identified as part of the learner's challenge topic. They are asked to consider what questions they would ask. They share their ideas in a class discussion.

Ways of working: You may wish to leave the activity as open as it is stated in the Learner's Skills Book or specify a relevant solution to a local issue.

Differentiation: Support learners by encouraging them to begin with questions that are designed to ascertain simple factual information. Challenge learners to develop a line of questioning, beginning with requests for clarification then extending to more probing questions. More probing questions could aim to find out to what extent the proposed course of action taken is appropriate to different needs, well-thought through and likely to meet the goal set.

Suggested answers:

Who?	What?	When?
Who will be responsible for carrying out the solution?	What is the total cost?	When will we see results?
Who has been consulted?	What is the main advantage of this solution?	When was this last tried out?

Where?	How?	Why?
Where has this solution been tried before?	How will we be affected?	Why has this solution not been tried here before?
Where is the closest place to here that this has been tried?	How will this affect younger children?	Why is this so much cheaper/better?

Starter activity (approx. 10–15 mins)

Good for: Learners to further develop their understanding of developing lines of questioning.

Activity: Read through the learning goals for this lesson with learners at the beginning of this activity. Learners take turns to take on the roles of Zara and Arun in a discussion of how appropriate/feasible/effective Arun's solution is.

Ways of working: Time should be allocated for learners to initially reflect on their role. Those playing Arun will need to be prepared to improvise some relevant detail to respond to those playing Zara's questions. These are shown in Downloadable 6.11. Those playing Arun will need to be prepared to follow up with further probing questions to ascertain relevant information from those playing Arun's answers. If you have a colleague available, you could act out Zara and Arun's discussion to model for your learners.

Differentiation: Support learners by listening in to discussion and prompting the 'Zaras', for example 'What could you ask them so that they could clarify that for you?' or prompting the 'Aruns', for example 'How could you explain why that is an effective response?' Challenge the 'Zaras' to ask more probing questions designed to find out to what extent the proposed course of action taken is appropriate to different needs, well-thought through and likely to meet the goal set. Challenge the 'Aruns' to develop their points so that the proposed course of action taken is clearly appropriate to different needs, well-thought through and likely to meet the goal set.

Suggested answers:

Zara: What other ways could we encourage? What about walking?

Arun: We could encourage walking; that would be welcome – but the focus of our campaign is cycling.

Zara: What reasons have been given for not cycling?

Arun: Distance is often given as a reason – but few people live more than 5 km from school and you soon get used to cycling that far.

Zara: Is this the same all over the world? Where does this research come from?

Arun: Cycling is very popular in Holland. It should be said that the weather there in winter is not ideal. Our climate might in fact be better.

Zara: Where is the closest place to here that this has been tried?

Arun: I don't know of anywhere locally – that doesn't mean we shouldn't try it out.

Zara: What's happening at the training event?

Arun: We've got coaches in so that you can learn about the skills you'll need if you haven't done a lot of riding before.

Main activity (approx. 20–25 mins)

Good for: Learners to apply the questioning/probing/elaborating/clarifying skills learnt in the Starter activity to their own issue.

Activity: Learners take turns to take on the roles of presenter and interviewer in a discussion of how appropriate/ feasible/ effective their solution is.

Ways of working: You may wish to leave the issue and solution open for them to develop from their previous work or specify a relevant solution to an issue (e.g. zoos) that they advocate.

Differentiation: See the Starter activity.

Suggested answers: Responses based on the school-grown vegetable project might be:

Q: Who will be responsible for carrying out the solution?

A: We will need the help of local gardening experts to help us develop our skills.

Q: Won't the children be involved?

A: The aim is that we develop the skills we need to take more responsibility.

Q: What will the cost be?

A: There will be some costs to build the raised beds and buy equipment – after that it may well be cheaper to grow vegetables than to buy them in.

Q: Won't the equipment be expensive?

A: We're hoping some can be donated.

For an example of annotation, see Downloadable 6.11.

Taking it further: Lesson 5

Encourage learners to talk in role as another person in order to advocate solutions to an issue (e.g. an urban planner advocating the creation of more cycle lanes as a solution to the issue of traffic congestion). This could take the form of a 'hot-seating' activity where the learner in the role of advocate faces questions from the class and answers them according to the perspective of the role they have adopted. The task of persuading a given audience will create opportunities to evaluate contexts when more formal registers and standard usage are necessary and appropriate, and when more informal registers can be effective.